Machine Embr...
ON DIFFICULT MAT...

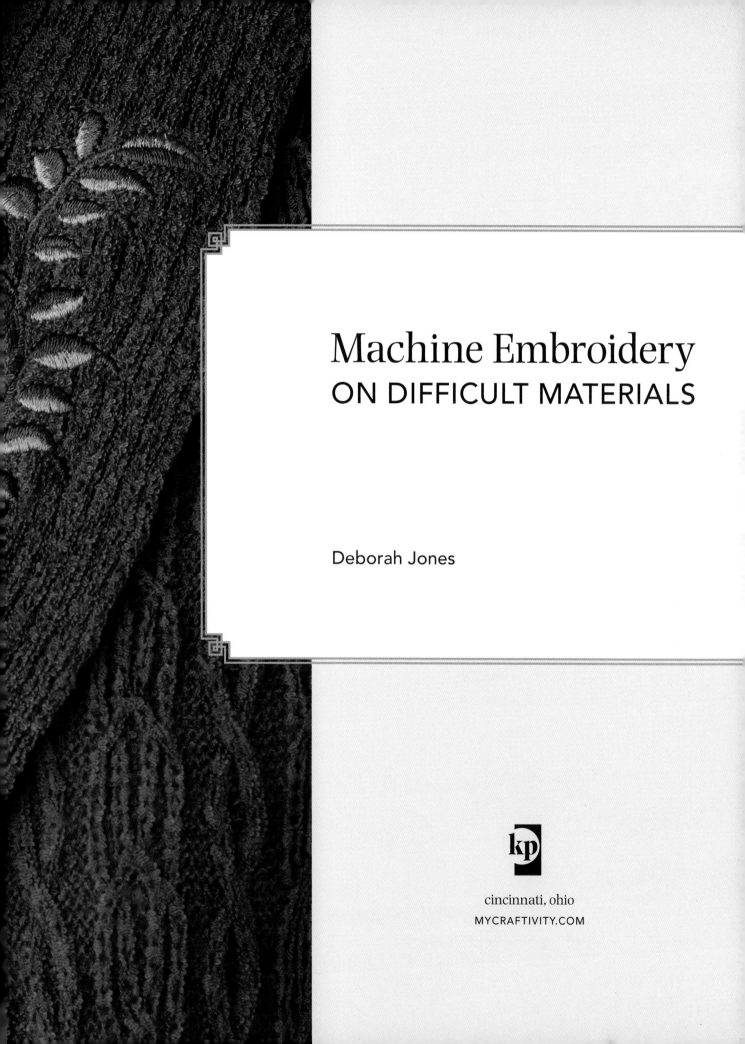

Machine Embroidery
ON DIFFICULT MATERIALS

Deborah Jones

kp

cincinnati, ohio
MYCRAFTIVITY.COM

Machine Embroidery on Difficult Materials Copyright © 2009 by Deborah Jones. Manufactured in China. All rights reserved. No part of this book may be reproduced in any form or by any electronic or mechanical means including information storage and retrieval systems without permission in writing from the publisher, except by a reviewer who may quote brief passages in a review. Published by Krause Publications, an imprint of F+W Media, Inc., 4700 East Galbraith Road, Cincinnati, Ohio, 45236. (800) 289-0963. First Edition.

media

13 12 11 10 09   5 4 3 2 1

DISTRIBUTED IN CANADA BY FRASER DIRECT

100 Armstrong Avenue

Georgetown, ON, Canada L7G 5S4

Tel: (905) 877-4411

DISTRIBUTED IN THE U.K. AND EUROPE BY DAVID & CHARLES

Brunel House, Newton Abbot, Devon, TQ12 4PU, England

Tel: (+44) 1626 323200, Fax: (+44) 1626 323319

Email: postmaster@davidandcharles.co.uk

DISTRIBUTED IN AUSTRALIA BY CAPRICORN LINK

P.O. Box 704, S. Windsor NSW, 2756 Australia

Tel: (02) 4577-3555

Library of Congress Cataloging in Publication Data

Jones, Deborah (Deborah Jones-Hurd)

Machine embroidery on difficult fabrics / Deborah Jones.

    p. cm.

Includes index.

ISBN 978-0-89689-654-3 (pbk. : alk. paper)

1. Embroidery, Machine. I. Title.

TT772.J66 2009

677'.77--dc22

                    2008034965

Designed by Michelle Thompson

Edited by Toni Toomey

Production edited by Amy Jeynes

Illustrations by Hayes Shanesy

Production coordinated by Matt Wagner

Needle illustrations courtesy of Ferd. Schmetz GMBH

Nonwoven stabilizer illustration (page 22) courtesy of QST Industries, Inc.)

About the Author

Deborah Jones has more than thirty years of professional experience in embroidery as a shop owner, production manager, and former editor for *Stitches* magazine.

Through articles and presentations, Deborah has taught thousands of embroiderers how to achieve greater success in their craft. She writes the "Ask the Expert" column for *Designs in Machine Embroidery* and is a regular contributor to *Impressions* magazine. She is also a popular speaker at embroidery events.

Currently, Deborah assists embroiderers through her website, www.embroiderycoach.com. She lives outside Dallas, Texas, with husband Bob and her beloved Silky Terriers and Anatolian Shepherds.

Acknowledgments

Special thanks to

Eileen Roche for her friendship, inspiration and encouragement.

Deegee Hitzfelder, whose friendship, sharp rotary blades and mat were indispensable.

Needle manufacturer Ferd. Schmetz GMBH for allowing use of their educational drawings of needles.

Bernina of America for use of the Bernina 730 and Artista software.

Brother International for the Innovis 4500D used in creating the projects in this book.

Sulky and Fred Drexler for the threads used in this book.

Artists Harry Jay, Shelley Brant-Levi and Bryant Royal for the wonderful artwork for the digitized designs.

Netemb.com for their excellent digitizing.

Tamara Evans, whose trusty serger makes a perfect rolled hem.

Melissa J. Thompson Maher, who helped me improve my writing skills.

My daughter, Cory Jones, a budding embroiderer who keeps me looking to the future of embroidery.

My husband, Bob Hurd, who went without meals, tended the dogs, and
was an all-around trouper while I was writing this book.

My sister, Becca Bowen, who always called just when I needed a break.

My editor Toni Toomey, who has a reverence for good technical information but also likes a good read.

My editor Amy Jeynes, who is a master of organization and detail.

Candy Wiza, acquisitions editor, who embraced the concept of this book.

Jay Staten, for her guidance and support.

This book is dedicated to
My father, Jack McClure, and my mentor, Shirley Landers, who
instilled in me a love of embroidery and who taught me the
beginnings of my embroidery skills.

And to
Embroiderers everywhere with your probing
questions and unending challenges.

Contents

When you love to machine embroider, you see all kinds of fabrics that you want to add special touches to. It's satisfying—and fun—to apply your vision to the kaleidoscope of fabric all around us. For many fabrics, your tried-and-true methods work, and the embroidery looks predictably wonderful.

But what about those other fabrics? You know, the ones that pucker and run, buckle and stretch, or completely bury your embroidery in mounds of plush pile or loops. These are the difficult materials that we want to master.

What does it mean to master a difficult fabric? For me it means that when I embroider it, the embroidery looks like it belongs there. In the case of a fabric with a soft hand, it should be possible to roll the embroidery between my hands, feeling an almost imperceptible difference between the embroidered areas and the rest of the fabric. On a stiff fabric, the embroidered area should not tear out or have highly visible holes around the embroidery. The appearance of the embroidery should be well formed and distinct, with proper stitch formation. The stitches should be laid into the fabric to look like they are part of the fabric, even when the design is intended to have a raised effect.

In short, embroidery should enhance its background, while the form and function of the base fabric is not altered. The embroidery should be of high quality, with appropriate tension balance. If you accomplish these things when applying embroidery, you have mastered the fabric. Is it possible to achieve good embroidery results on any fabric? For me, so far the answer is yes. With enough time and tinkering, I have been able to master any fabric I took on, eventually. The toughest opponent? Probably Taslon nylon used in race car uniforms. Because this was a production job that had to be completed, giving up was not an option. Solving embroidery challenges with difficult fabrics is a matter of identifying the challenges and applying logic to solve them. Let's look at some underlying reasons why some fabrics try our patience.

FABRIC CHARACTERISTICS
AFFECT EMBROIDERY

One of the wonderful things about embroidering is seeing how the design looks when applied to various types of fabric. The same design can look completely different when applied to a textured surface or a smooth one, to a shiny or a matte finish.

Ironically, one of the vexing things about doing embroidery is successfully applying embroidery to different fabrics. Indeed, some fabrics may be successfully embroidered using a variety of techniques, while others have a more narrow tolerance for the embroidery process.

It's possible that any of the components may need to be changed from what is considered standard for a general category of fabric. The weight or type of stabilizer, needle size and point type, and even the holding method are all candidates to be evaluated for every fabric.

EVALUATING SAMPLE STITCH-OUTS

It's advisable to do a sample stitch-out on any unfamiliar fabric type. If you see problems, you can evaluate them to uncover the cause, and then apply changes to correct it. Sound complicated? Not really. There is a finite set of variables, and you can try several remedies if necessary. With a little practice, you will be able to accurately interpret the symptoms that you see. You will also learn that different factors can be responsible for similar symptoms, so try not to be automatic in your assessments.

For example, if you see puckering, the cause could be too much density in the design (fig. 1-A), an insufficient or inappropriate stabilizer, improper hooping, or improper needle point. You may wonder where to begin your troubleshooting. Always begin with the simplest solution first. Here is a situation that illustrates the process. Imagine this: While embroidering a lightweight woven fabric you see puckering around the edges of the design (fig. 2).

Fig. 1-A. A design that stitches well on one fabric may have too much density, or too many stitches, for a lighter fabric. Here, there is too much density, making the design too stiff.

Fig. 1-B. It is possible to edit designs in embroidery software to be suitable for any fabric. The density is correct for this fabric. You can see here that the design is almost as supple as the fabric.

In this situation, the simplest thing is to add stabilizer. While not as supportive as a stabilizer that is hooped in with the fabric, you can add one or more layers of stabilizer while stitching. "Floating" is a term that refers to the practice of sliding one or more pieces of stabilizer between the hoop and the machine table (fig. 3). Even though it is not hooped in, you should be able to tell whether hooping additional stabilizer in with the next item will provide the needed support. Stop the machine and slide one or two layers of crisp tear-away stabilizer and restart the machine. Watch the stitching carefully to see if it appears that the puckering has been diminished.

Fig. 2. If you detect puckering while stitching a design, try adding stabilizer by "floating" it (fig. 3).

The second simplest thing to try can be tested while continuing to stitch the initial test. You can change to a different needle point type or blade size. In this instance, a sharp needle will penetrate the fabric best, yet many, if not most, embroiderers never use a sharp point for embroidery. The standard embroidery needles sold in the United States have a light ball point, designated SES. This needle point type has come to be regarded as suitable for both woven and knit fabrics, yet for lightweight or tightly woven fabric, a sharp point needle frequently eliminates puckering symptoms.

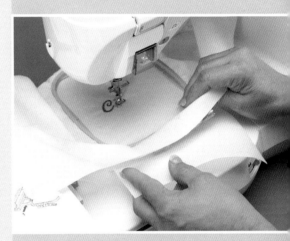

Fig. 3. "Float" stabilizer by placing one or more pieces between hooped item and machine bed to diminish puckering that is detected while stitching.

HOOPING TECHNIQUE

For most fabrics, the traditional two-ring hoop provides the most secure hold (fig. 4). If you are using an alternative method, ask yourself whether it is possible or desirable to attempt the fabric using a two-ring hoop. If not, is there a more secure method available? Holding methods are discussed in detail in Chapter 4.

PROGRAMMING DESIGN PROPERTIES

Programming may be the last element to work with simply because you can't change it during the initial stitch-out. If you have tried changes with the other elements, making changes to the design data itself could be the magic bullet. The most important areas to look at are suitability of stitch density, stitch length, and underlay characteristics. There is more information on each of these throughout the book.

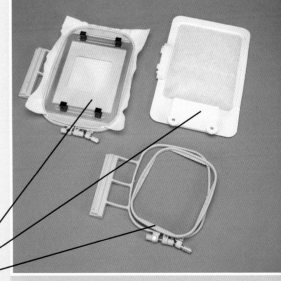

Magna-Hoop
Hoop-It-All self adhesive holder
Two-ring hoop

Fig. 4. The traditional two-ring hoop provides the best grip and tensioning for most fabrics. Alternative holding methods may be needed for some fabric types.

CHAPTER ONE

The Fabrics

Some fabrics are more difficult than others to embroider. Nonetheless, as this book will show you, the proper combination of components and techniques can be used to embroider even the difficult fabrics reliably.

KNITTED FABRICS: THE STRETCH FACTOR

Stretch fabrics can be some of the most challenging ones to machine embroider, but they are a great example of how easy it is to get consistently good results by using logic and following a few simple guidelines. Yet this category possibly has the most variables and requires the most careful consideration of all the components.

There are many varieties of stretch fabrics, including everything from fine jersey knits to two-way stretch fabrics to bulky sweater knits. Despite their differences, they have some things in common. Stretch fabrics have a natural "memory" that causes the yarn to try to return to its original location when moved by stitching.

You may have enjoyed initial success with your embroidery on knits, only to be taken completely by surprise by a project having puckering or misaligned outline stitching. The reason for the difference could be as simple as the design itself.

A single-color design similar to the Nike swoosh logo could be successfully embroidered on a knit fabric with almost any stabilizer, including a lightweight tear-away. But if you try embroidering a large, multi-color design using the same stabilizer on the same fabric, the result is likely to be poor quality embroidery.

Even if a design is properly digitized for knit fabrics, appropriate support must be supplied to the fabric. A lightweight tear-away stabilizer cannot provide sufficient support to a lightweight knit when a substantial number of stitches are applied.

Smooth and Textured Knits

A one-piece baby romper and your favorite sweatshirt both have a fairly smooth face when compared to more bulky or open knits. Yet these examples of smooth-face knits have very different properties for embroidery purposes. The baby garment is likely knitted with finer yarn, in a jersey knit construction, which is very smooth on one side and slightly rougher on the other. The sweatshirt probably has a ribbed surface and a fleece back, which adds body (fig. 1-1).

Principles for Embroidering on Smooth, Lightweight Knits

The reason that we like to wear this type of knit is precisely the same reason there are challenges associated with embroidering it—it has movement and stretch. These characteristics give us the pleasure associated with comfort clothing like T-shirts and sweatshirts. These fabrics are also generally soft to the touch, with high drapeability. It is important that we change those characteristics as little as possible when applying embroidery.

Knits are made from yarn, which has a memory, or a tendency to return to its original shape after the embroidery hoop has been removed. You can imagine that if embroidery thread has displaced these yarns, it is impossible for them to return where the embroidery thread has been applied into the fabric.

During embroidery, the hoop keeps the knit taut, but when the hoop is removed, the knit may curl around the edges of the embroidery. If you see this symptom, it is probably caused by one of two things. The knit may have been stretched too much during hooping (figs. 1-2A and 1-2B), and the yarn's memory is causing it to return to its position before it was stretched. Another cause could be that the knit was pushed out of its original location by the embroidery stitches (fig. 1-6B) because the design has too many stitches in a concentrated area or an insufficient stabilizer layer.

Smooth-face knits that are commonly used in T-shirt construction vary in weight from so-called "tissue" T-shirts, about a 3.2 (91 gram) weight, to heavyweight shirts made from fabric weighing over 6 ounces (170 grams). These weights are derived from the number of ounces in a square yard of a specific fabric. Sweatshirt fleece can vary from 7.75 ounces (220 grams) to over twice that weight. How does this affect the embroidery process?

One important area is the use of stabilizers for knits. The usual recommendation for stabilizer type for any knit fabric is a cut-away

Fig. 1-1. There are many different types and weights of knits. This sweatshirt knit (top) is not as smooth as the jersey knit (bottom), but it has more body, which could make it easier to embroider.

variety. Cut-away stabilizer can vary from 1 to 2.5 ounces (28 to 71 grams) in weight. Lighter-weight knits need to have more stabilization, but that doesn't translate to heavier-weight stabilizer. Pairing a heavyweight stabilizer with a lightweight knit may well eliminate puckering and shifting, but the resulting embroidery would be hard and stiff.

A better choice is a lightweight cut-away stabilizer that has been engineered to have minimal stretch. It is possible to use a stabilizer of only 1 to 1.5 ounces (28 to 43 grams) to stabilize a design having 10,000 to 12,000 stitches on a lightweight smooth-face knit. To be successful, however, the design must have appropriate stitch density, and correct hooping technique must be used.

Fig. 1-2A. This shirt was pulled too tightly during hooping.

Fig. 1-2B. Even though the embroidery may look unpuckered in the hoop, once unhooped, the yarn's "memory" causes it to regain its original position, now occupied by the embroidery. The result is puckering around the design.

15

Principles for Embroidering on Textured Knits

Sweater or cable-knit fabrics are often made with thicker yarn resulting in a knit with more loft. This is a knit that may compress as well as be pushed and pulled during the embroidery process.

Multidirectional stretch fabric is used in the construction of items that must stretch to be worn. Symptoms associated with stretching during embroidery are greatly exaggerated with this type of knit. Special methods must be employed to control the stretch factor and successfully apply high-quality embroidery to this fabric type.

For most knits, it's best to control stretching of the fabric during embroidery. Generally, you should use techniques to minimize stretching during the hooping process and during the application of embroidery.

One notable exception is when a knit garment will be stretched tightly across the body, such as a swim suit or bike shorts. Under these circumstances, multidirectional stretch fabrics should be stretched slightly while hooping to help assure that holes will not appear around the embroidery when worn (figs. 1-3A and 1-3B).

Fig. 1-3A. Properly embroidered two-way stretch knit may look peculiar when not being worn.

Fig. 1-3B. Slight stretching during hooping helps avoid holes around the embroidery when stretched across the wearer's body.

16

Programming Design Properties for Knits

In general terms, designs for knits should have relatively light density and, where practical, longer stitch-length values in large areas of coverage. These techniques help the embroidery to have a more relaxed appearance and avoid the tendency to draw in or pucker. Making stitches slightly longer by altering the default stitch-length setting can help create softer embroidery by placing fewer stitches in the fabric (fig. 1-4).

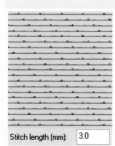
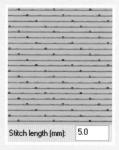

Stitch length (mm): 3.0   Stitch length (mm): 5.0

Fig. 1-4. A shorter stitch length (above, left) means more stitches are needed to cover an area. By lengthening the stitches slightly (above, right), you reduce the number of stitches needed, and the result is softer embroidery with less puckering.

Fig. 1-5. Underlay stitching is the light layer of stitches that is applied before the final layer.

Fig. 1-6A. On unstable fabrics, start with a layer of underlay stitching to tack the fabric to the stabilizer, then embroider the final shape.

Underlay

Underlay stitching is a light-density layer that is applied to the fabric before the final layer is stitched (fig. 1-5). It serves several functions, including adding loft, dimension, and structure. For knits, it serves another very important function—it tacks the face fabric to the stabilizer layer beneath (fig. 1-6A). This makes the knit much less likely to shift, bunch or be pushed. When no underlay is present, the soft knit can be easily pushed in the direction of stitching, creating a bubble of fabric that can become trapped (fig. 1-6B). Underlay is a necessary component in programming for knits.

Fig. 1-6B. If you skip underlay stitching on unstable fabrics, the stitching may push the fabric, creating a bubble.

17

Pull Compensation

Pull compensation is a programming technique that helps to reduce the effects of the stitches pushing and pulling on the unstable knit fabric (fig. 1-7). Most software programs add width to design elements using a percentage value to counteract the pull on the fabric. In effect, it makes the object, for example, 2 percent larger to compensate for the fabric pulling in. This can help the outlines be placed in the proper place on the design, instead of having a gap between the design element and its outline.

In embroidery software, you may need to select between two types of pull compensation, *absolute* and *percentage*. Both types add to the design in the direction of the stitching to compensate for the inward pull on the fabric. As their names imply, for absolute, add a specific value measured in embroidery points, and in percentage, add an amount based on the percentage of the size of the object. Generally, I use percentage for lettering and absolute for objects.

DENSELY WOVEN FABRICS: THE FRICTION FACTOR

You may have to think back to sixth grade science class to refresh your memory about friction. As you recall, friction is a force that is created when objects rub against each other. It's natural that friction is created by the needle rubbing against the fabric, and there is even more natural friction when the fabric is difficult to penetrate, as with tightly woven fabrics. This friction can cause the thread to fray and break (fig. 1-8).

Nylon and polyester are examples of tough synthetic fabrics that present embroidery challenges, yet some natural fibers can be equally difficult. For example, silk is an interesting testament to the strength and toughness of natural fibers. Early Mongol warriors wore a silk garment under their armor to stop arrows from deeply penetrating the body. The arrow could be popped out by pulling on two sides of the silk. To be successful embroidering on dense fabrics, remember that the effect of friction is magnified greatly as compared to other fabric types.

Fig. 1-7. An outline that looks perfect on your computer screen may be off-register when stitched because of the pull on the fabric. Changing the pull compensation values in your embroidery software will help to counteract pulling.

Fig. 1-8. Friction caused this thread to break, as evidenced by its frayed appearance.

UNFABRICS: THE PERFORATION FACTOR

Embroidery surfaces that aren't fabrics. such as leather and vinyl, also present friction issues. With these "unfabrics," the friction may be so severe that it causes frequent thread breaks (fig. 1-8). In fact, these thread breaks may be caused when the thread becomes trapped inside the material and can't exit on the upstroke of the needle. It is necessary to use the most appropriate needle type for these materials to overcome the effects of friction and the tendency of these fabrics to be cut or perforated by the needle. Unfortunately, embroiderers working on leather or vinyl often use needles recommended for sewing *seams* on leather and vinyl. These needles have cutting points (fig. 1-9) and are designed to help a sewing machine make very straight seams. When a cutting needle is used to place stitches in very close proximity for embroidery, there can be too much perforation of the embroidery surface. This is why many embroiderers believe that all embroidery on leather or leather-like materials will punch out like a paper doll. When the proper needle is used on garment-quality leather, this is not a risk.

It is also necessary to use stabilization techniques with leather and vinyl to control stretching. Leather and vinyl stretch when embroidery is applied, and these materials should be treated as unstable backgrounds in many aspects.

SLICK AND SHEER FABRICS: THE SLIPPAGE FACTOR

Lightweight fabrics come in many varieties, and some are easily embroidered. One of the most common challenges with sheer fabrics is slippage in the hoop, which can result in puckering and misalignment of design elements. Traditional hooping methods are frequently not adequate to control lightweight and slippery fabrics.

Tensions may also need to be adjusted for lightweight fabrics. A light bobbin tension allows more thread on the reverse side of the embroidery than normal (fig. 1-10). For example, a sheer fabric that is easily pulled inward when stitches are applied may require a very light bobbin tension.

As you can see, there are many variables when embroidering different fabrics. The next chapter will discuss how to choose the right embroidery components for successful embroidery on challenging fabrics.

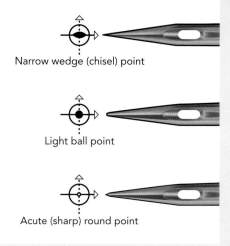

Narrow wedge (chisel) point

Light ball point

Acute (sharp) round point

Fig. 1-9. Cutting needles, such as the Narrow Wedge Point (top), were designed to help make straight seams. They should not be used for embroidery because of the close proximity of embroidery stitches. The Wedge Point's hole size (indicated by the shape inside the circle at top left) and sharp edges can damage the material or previously applied embroidery stitches. Notice the large, long hole created by the Narrow Wedge point versus the smaller holes created by the Light Ball and the Acute Round.

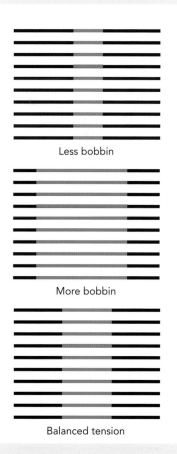

Less bobbin

More bobbin

Balanced tension

Fig. 1-10. The bobbin tension for machine embroidery on slick and sheer fabrics should allow a higher-than-usual ratio of bobbin thread to top thread, as shown in the center example.

CHAPTER TWO

Choosing Embroidery Components:

Stabilizers

Stabilizers provide the foundation for the embroidery stitch. In fact, in some cases, you are stitching on the stabilizer, and the fabric just gets in the way!

Many years ago, when I started doing machine embroidery, there were no stabilizers made just for embroidery. We used many types of materials, including interfacings intended for garment construction. For tear away, we even resorted to unusual materials including a type of coarse, folded commercial paper towel.

Today, this seems almost comical because there are so many types of stabilizers made specifically for embroidery use. Yet because there are so many different brands and styles, it can be difficult to remember the purpose that each is intended for. Regardless which type is best for your purpose, never let price deter you from choosing the best stabilizer for your foundation. There is no economy in using a cheap stabilizer.

The generally accepted recommendation is to use tear-away stabilizers for woven fabrics and cut-away stabilizers for knits. Of course this is a general guideline, and with experience, you may vary from it. Even if you are experienced in machine embroidery, you may not rely completely on either experience or rules to choose stabilizers. Aside from fabric type, there are other variables that factor into stabilizer selection, such as number and concentration of stitches in the design, amount of detail, and holding method. Think about each project independently and apply logic to that specific situation.

For example, a limp fabric will tend to pull inward with a soft stabilizer, so logic says to try a stabilizer with a crisp hand. On the other hand, a crisp fabric with a heavy design may benefit from a soft tear-away that can provide support throughout the embroidery without punching out and tearing away from the embroidery. Unfamiliar fabrics may require a couple of experiments, but with each test you will become more confident about what your final result will be. Let's look at the various stabilizers and how to apply logic to select the one most appropriate to each project.

Stabilizer weight is measured in ounces, representing the weight of a square yard of a particular stabilizer. Embroidery stabilizers range in weight from 1 to 3 ounces (28 to 85 grams). If you don't know what weight of stabilizers you use, begin to take note of it so you will become more familiar with the characteristics of each weight. It is also important to stitch test swatches with new stabilizers that you want to try. It simply isn't possible to predict the performance of a stabilizer by feeling it.

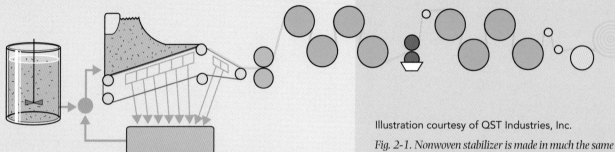

Illustration courtesy of QST Industries, Inc.

Fig. 2-1. Nonwoven stabilizer is made in much the same way as paper, by adding fibers to a vat of liquid and then spreading to dry.

NONWOVEN STABILIZERS

As the name indicates, these are not woven but formed. There are several methods of creating nonwoven fabrics and stabilizers, but for the purpose of creating a high-quality embroidery stabilizer, the best method is very similar to the one used to make paper (fig. 2-1). In basic terms, fibers, often rayon, polyester, and cellulose, are mixed together in a liquid solution. The fibers may be short or long, or a combination of short and long, depending on the desired properties of the stabilizer. For example, cut-away stabilizers are made from longer fibers, and most tear-away is made from shorter fibers. The fibers are bonded with a binding agent, and silicone is added for smoother stitching. Then the fibers are removed from the solution with a screen, forming a material that is even in weight and uniform in all directions.

Tear-away stabilizers made by this "wet-laid" method tears with equal ease in all directions and is referred to as nondirectional. If you see the words "wet-laid" in the description of a stabilizer brand, you know that it is a high-quality product. This type of high-quality stabilizer is made in a variety of weights, so you can choose the appropriate weight and use a single layer. Less expensive nonwoven stabilizers are often made from other methods that can result in an uneven concentration of fibers. There are thick and thin spots that can cause stitching problems. They also have a tendency to stretch in one direction, requiring use of multiple layers laid at opposing angles in the hoop. This cheaper variety is much less suitable for embroidery and is not worth any savings in price.

TEAR-AWAY STABILIZERS

Nonwoven tear-away stabilizers are designed to be pulled away from completed embroidery, requiring no trimming. To avoid stressing the stitches during the removal process, use the proper weight of stabilizer, place a finger near the edge of the embroidery to support it, and remove only one layer of stabilizer at a time (figs. 2-2A and 2-2B).

Tear-away can have a crisp or soft hand and be heavy or light in weight. Generally speaking, tear-away is best suited to stable woven fabrics, such as poplin, broadcloth, oxford, and so on. If you are an experienced embroiderer, you may have success matching tear-away with certain knits. For example, sweatshirts that have good body can be successfully embroidered with softer tear-away products that have more resistance to perforation. These softer tear-away products are made of a blend of long and short fibers and hold together much better than crisper tear-away products.

Even though today's stabilizers are engineered to allow use of a single layer of the proper weight, you might choose to use multiple layers of a lightweight 1-ounce (28-gram) variety. These layers are removed one at a time so that even a single row of running stitches will not be stressed during removal.

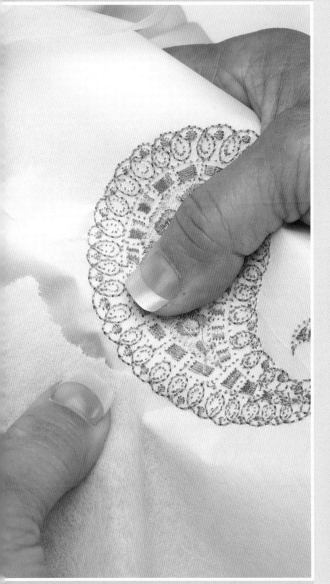

Fig. 2-2A. Remove the tear-away one layer at a time.

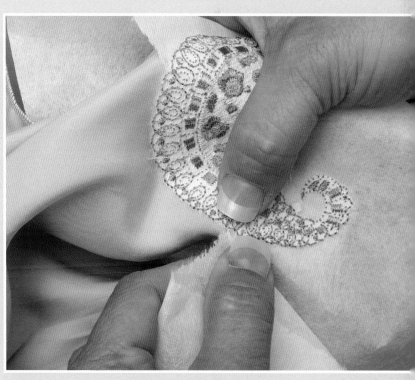

Fig. 2-2B. Hold the embroidery close to the edge while removing tear-away stabilizer to avoid distorting the stitches.

CUT-AWAY STABILIZERS

This stabilizer type is recommended for knits and other unstable fabric types. As the name implies, this stabilizer is trimmed away from the edge of the embroidery after you remove the fabric from the hoop. The stabilization lasts not just while you are stitching, but for the life of the garment. In certain situations, tear-away stabilizers can break down and stop furnishing support even before you have completed stitching a detailed design on an unstable fabric.

For best support, be sure that your cut-away stabilizer is hooped in with the fabric and that it extends from all edges of your hoop (figs. 2-3A and 2-3B). Generally, there is no need to choose a thick cut away because there are many light, soft and reliable cut-away products. Most are nonwoven, but one unique product that provides superior stability and softness is made by a special method called the "spun bond" method. This stabilizer is sold by several companies under different names such as No Show Mesh and PolyMesh. The name PolyMesh is widely recognized, but my industry sources tell me that the fiber content is sometimes nylon. Spun-bond stabilizer can be identified by its characteristic waffle imprint (fig. 2-4). Its popularity has caused it to be made in several weights and colors and in fusible and nonfusible varieties. It has virtually no stretch or shrinkage and is popular because its translucent qualities mean it won't show through your garments.

Fig. 2-3A. Improperly hooped stabilizer. Edges do not extend past the hoop on all sides.

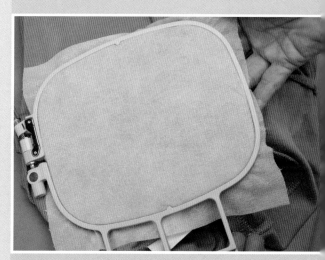

Fig. 2-3B. Stabilizer should be flat and smooth, extending from all edges of your hoop.

Fig. 2-4. There is a visible difference between a polymesh type stabilizer made using the spun bond method of manufacture and the traditional nonwoven cut-away.

You can also use certain fabrics as cut-away stabilizers. Inexpensive fabrics such as polyester organza have long been favored by free-motion embroiderers for stabilizing embroidery on sweaters and other open-weave items (fig. 2-6). They also work well with computerized machines. You can purchase these fabrics in colors to match the garment, eliminating stabilizer show-through on these difficult items. If you choose a fabric that has any tendency to shrink, be sure to prewash it before using in your project.

Trim cut-away stabilizer about ¼ inch (6mm) away from the embroidery (fig. 2-5). Trimming too far away may cause an impression of the stabilizer to be seen through the fabric. Trimming too close can result in a sunken appearance around the embroidery.

SPECIALTY STABILIZERS
Fusible
There are fusible, meaning iron-on, stabilizers available in both cut-away and tear-away categories. A fusible stabilizer can be helpful in preventing distortion of the fabric during hooping. When using a fusible, always test for suitability of the adhesive's melting point with your fabric type.

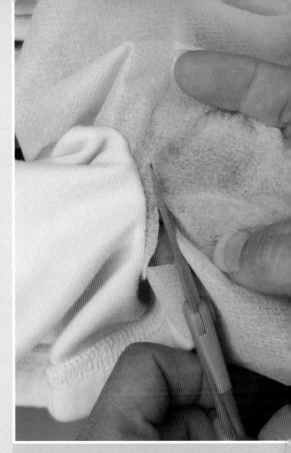

Fig. 2-5. Trim cut-away stabilizer about ¼ inch (6mm) away from the embroidery. Leaving too wide a margin of stabilizer will result in a visible impression on the face of the garment, while trimming too close may cause a sunken appearance around the design.

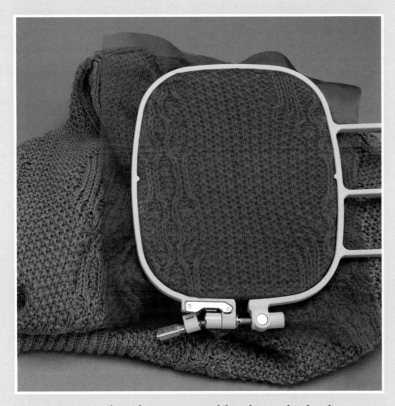

Fig. 2-6. Organza can be used as a cut-away stabilizer that matches the color of open-weave knits.

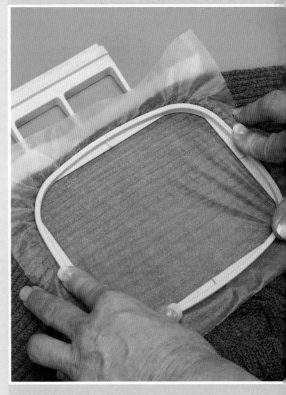

Fig. 2-7. You can also use water soluble stabilizer with a bulky knit.

Self-Adhesive

This type of stabilizer consists of a sticky coating on a paper substrate, covered with another topping paper. The topping paper is removed to expose the sticky surface, and the item to be embroidered is adhered to the surface. Self-adhesive stabilizers are frequently used for items that are hard to hoop or too small to hoop, or that could show hoop marks.

This stabilizer variety may be hooped or attached to a specialty fixture. If you hoop self-adhesive stabilizer in your regular hoop, be sure to remove it as soon as your project is finished to avoid adhesive build-up. You can also use the method shown in figures 2-9A and 2-9B to avoid adhesive residue on your hoop. There are many tear-away self-adhesive products, but just as with other tear-aways, these are not generally suited to high stitch count designs on unstable fabrics.

Fig. 2-8. Commercially available toppings can be used to permanently control pile fabrics and to help mask a starkly contrasting fabric color, allowing the thread color to provide good coverage.

Fig. 2-9A. Hoop the self-adhesive stabilizer with the release paper topping facing up. Score this paper topping with a pin.

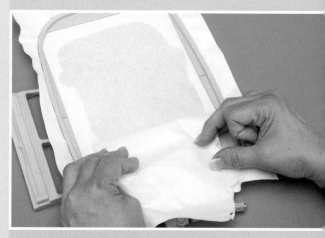

Fig. 2-9B. After scoring, pull away the release paper to expose the sticky surface only in the embroidery area, keeping your hoop free of sticky residue.

Fig. 2-10A. To remove water-soluble stabilizer, first pull most of it away, using care not to stress the work.

Fig. 2-10B. Then mist to remove remaining stabilizer from the inside of the design.

Permanent Toppings

A permanent topping in a variety of colors is available under the trade name of Dry Cover-Up (fig. 2-8). This type of topping permanently controls pile fabrics and masks highly contrasting fabrics from showing through your embroidery. Permanent topping does not dissolve, so it should be torn away after the underlay stitching is applied so that the top layer of stitches hides it completely.

Water Soluble

Water-soluble stabilizers are usually used on top of textured fabrics or towels to eliminate the tendency of pile or loops to come through the embroidery stitches. Even lightly textured fabrics such as piqué knit and sweatshirt knit benefit from a layer of lightweight (20 micron) water-soluble topping to provide a smooth embroidery surface. This helps create crisper, cleaner edges on columns of stitching because the needle can enter the fabric on a smooth flat surface, rather than falling into a valley.

Water-soluble products can also be used below the fabric in your hoop as a stabilizer. When embroidering batiste, lawn, organza, organdy or other sheer fabrics, you can use a midweight (approximately 35 micron) water-soluble product beneath the fabric. It makes a better choice than a standard tear-away, because even very lightweight standard tear-away is always visible through the fabric. If you don't have midweight water-soluble on hand, you can substitute multiple layers of lightweight water-soluble bonded together with an iron (figs. 2-11A–2-11C).

Even if you don't always place the water-soluble stabilizer in the hoop when using it on top of the fabric, you should always hoop it in completely when using it on the bottom as a stabilizer.

After embroidery is complete, just pull away the water-soluble product and, if desired, moisten or steam the remaining bits to remove them (figs. 2-10A and 2-10B). Either way, this clear stabilizer is invisible and will be gone after the first washing.

Add fabric softener to a spray bottle with a fine mist sprayer at the ratio of 12 parts water to one part fabric softener to aid in removal. Pretest for suitability for your fabric, whatever removal method you choose.

Heat Soluble

Similar in use and appearance to water-soluble stabilizers, these transparent-film stabilizers may be used with certain fabrics that can't be moistened. Compatible fabrics must be able to withstand temperatures from 260 to 300 degrees Fahrenheit (126 to 148 degrees Celsius).

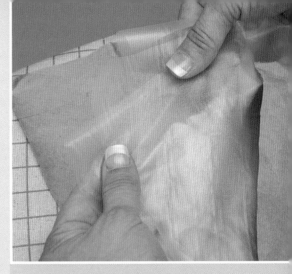

Fig. 2-11A. Place multiple layers of lightweight water-soluble stabilizer between two sheets of brown paper bag.

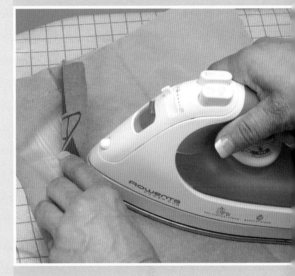

Fig. 2-11B. Iron the layers between pieces of brown paper bags.

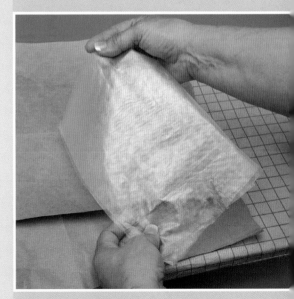

Fig. 2-11C. The layers of lightweight water-soluble stabilizer are now joined into a new, heavier sheet.

CHAPTER THREE

Choosing Embroidery Components:

Needles

Next to your stabilizer selection, your needle selection is probably the single most important component in the embroidery process, particularly on difficult fabrics. Some fabrics are more forgiving than others, so we may forget how important this aspect can be with certain fabric types. After all, if needle types weren't important, needle companies would not have developed the wide array of point and blade types available to us. The fabric type and thread type each have an important impact on needle selection.

Variances in physical characteristics of needles, such as point and blade types, are designed to give optimum performance on specific fabrics. Indeed, there may be slight differences between various manufacturers' needles of the same type. For this reason, you may find that a particular brand works best in your machine. Your dealer may recommend that you use a particular brand of needle because of subtle differences in the length of the scarf, distance from the eye to the tip, or other physical characteristics.

SEWING NEEDLE OR EMBROIDERY NEEDLE?

Let's identify what makes an embroidery needle different from a sewing needle. Most noticeably, the eye is larger than the eye on a standard sewing needle of the same size (fig. 3-1). This enlarged eye is designed to reduce friction on delicate decorative threads, reducing thread breakage.

The trade-off is that this larger eye makes the needle itself more susceptible to breakage because there is less metal in the eye area. The long groove that runs down the front of the blade is wider than on a similar size standard sewing needle (fig. 3-1). This modification is again made to reduce friction by better accommodating the larger diameter of embroidery thread.

Finally, the scarf, or small scoop on the back of the needle, is an important part of the embroidery needle. Found on the back of the needle, just above the eye, it helps to prevent skipped stitches (fig. 3-2). Certain needle types have a specially shaped scarf that helps to reliably form the embroidery stitch.

ROUND SHANK AND FLAT SHANK STYLES

Household embroidery machines use a flat shank needle. The purpose of the flat shank is to precisely position the needle in relation to the sewing hook. Commercial and crossover multi-needle embroidery machines have a round shank.

The round shank needles are available in many more varieties for the purpose of embroidery than the flat shank style. For this reason, it is sometimes preferable to embroider with a flat shank sewing needle that has the best characteristics for your fabric type than to use an inappropriate embroidery needle.

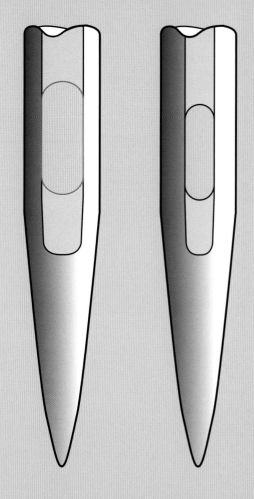

Fig. 3-1. The eye on an embroidery needle (left) is larger than that on a sewing needle (right), allowing the thread to flow more freely.

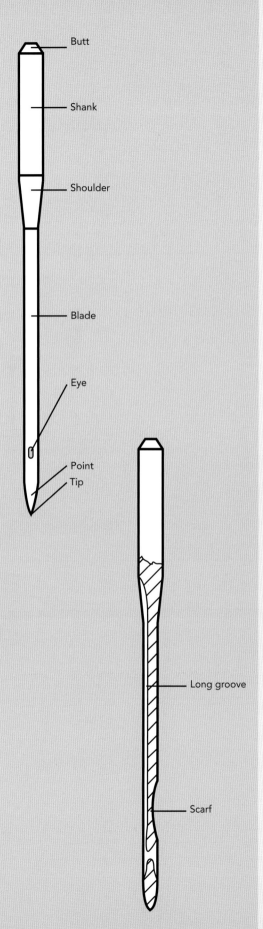

Butt

Shank

Shoulder

Blade

Eye

Point

Tip

Long groove

Scarf

Fig. 3-2. The parts of the needle.

THE BLADE

When deciding which needle to use, the first thing some of us consider is the size, such as size 75/11 or 90/14. Have you ever wondered why there are two numbers in this designation? The first number is the European designation, and refers to the actual measurement of the blade diameter. For example, a size 80 needle has a .80 mm blade width. The second number, such as 11 or 14, is an Asian numbering system, also formerly used by Singer.

Use a finer blade on more finely woven or knitted fabrics, which is possible to do when embroidering thanks to the wider groove and elongated eye in embroidery needles. They were created to accommodate embroidery thread in a smaller blade size.

THE EYE AND GROOVE

The eye of the embroidery needle is about twice the size of the same size sewing needle. In other words, the size of the eye in a size 70/10 embroidery needle is similar in size to the eye in a size 90/14 sewing needle. The groove on the front of the needle is also wider.

The larger eye and groove reduce friction on the thread, allowing it to flow more freely with fewer thread breaks. The eye and groove are also highly polished to remove burrs or rough spots that could damage the thread. This is particularly important for use with delicate rayon and other decorative threads. When stitching with very fine thread, such as a size 50 or 60, used for delicate details or tiny letters, make sure that the size of the needle and eye are suitable. You will not achieve the desired precision stitching that led you to select a small thread if you use too large a needle. With too large a needle, the groove will not be able to do a proper job of guiding the thread, and the thread will not be controlled properly in the eye.

There is a type of embroidery needle made especially for use with metallic thread. It has an even larger, specially-shaped eye that reduces stress on delicate metallic threads. This larger eye is very important when embroidering with metallic threads, so if you can't get a needle designed for metallic thread, use a needle made for large thread, such as a topstitching needle.

THE POINT

The point of the needle (fig. 3-3) is designed to penetrate the fabric without damaging it. The needle point also works with the blade size to create a hole of appropriate size for the thread to enter and escape. The point must also enter the fabric easily so it does not deflect (fig. 3-4) when it contacts the fabric, which could cause the needle to strike the metal surrounding the hole in the needle plate.

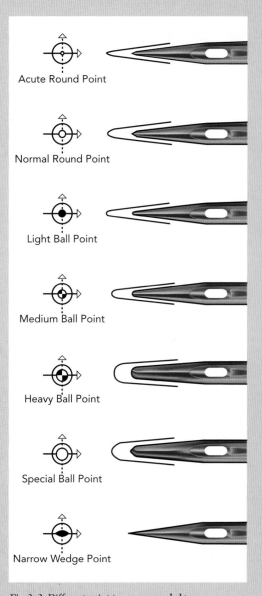

Acute Round Point

Normal Round Point

Light Ball Point

Medium Ball Point

Heavy Ball Point

Special Ball Point

Narrow Wedge Point

Fig. 3-3. Different point types are needed to penetrate cleanly and without fabric damage on a variety of fabric types.

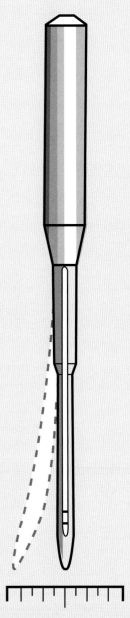

Fig. 3-4. The point of the needle must enter the fabric easily so that it does not deflect when it contacts the fabric.

There are two fundamental types of needles used for sewing and embroidering: sharp point and ball point. There are other types of specialty needles intended for specific fabric types when sewing on them, but not necessarily when embroidering on them. For example, the cutting-point needles used for some sewing applications are not recommended for embroidery, for two reasons. First, the highly concentrated needle penetrations required for embroidery would damage the embroidery surface. Second, the cutting tips would damage the embroidery itself (fig. 3-5).

Sharp point needles, also called round point, are generally used for woven fabrics. For very densely woven fabrics, an acute round may be used. An acute round has a more slender tip and is designed for easier penetration of tightly woven fabrics. This is the point type used for needles designed for stitching on microfiber fabrics. If an acute round point embroidery needle cannot be found, it may be preferable to select a sewing needle with this point type rather than using an embroidery needle. In some cases, the point type is more important to embroidery success than the characteristics of the embroidery needle.

There is more variety of needle points in round shank embroidery needles than in the flat shank variety. That means that the crossover type machine or semicommercial, multi-needle machines that use round shank needles may have more versions of true embroidery style needles available. If you are working with certain fabric characteristics where point type is critical, and the point type is not available in an embroidery needle, experiment with a sewing needle with that point type. Chances are very good that it may produce a better result than an embroidery needle with an incorrect point type.

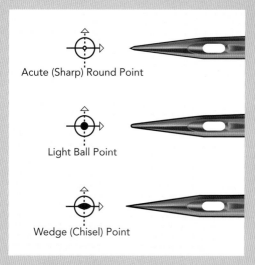

Acute (Sharp) Round Point

Light Ball Point

Wedge (Chisel) Point

Fig. 3-5. Wedge or chisel point needles are appropriate for making a seam in leather, but their large hole size makes them unsuitable for the close proximity of embroidery stitches in leather.

NEEDLE COATINGS

Most needles are chromium plated to enhance durability as well as appearance. You may have heard about needles with a titanium coating. They are more expensive than chromium-plated needles, but are they worth it? In a word, probably. They last longer and create less friction. Less friction could translate to less thread breakage and other stitching advantages.

The main reason needles need to be changed is that the point wears down (fig. 3-6). This is called attrition. This happens very quickly with abrasive fabrics and with fine point types. The points on titanium coated needles have five to seven times less attrition as chromium-plated needles, yet they don't cost five to seven times the price. Availability is still limited to the most popular sizes and types of needles, but it is available for the size 75/11 light ball point. Needles of this size and point type are by far the most popular size sold for embroidery use.

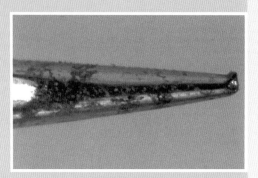

Fig. 3-6. Needle points can become flattened and burred through overuse, resulting in damage to fabrics.

CHANGING NEEDLES

Now for the question most often asked about needles —how often should they be changed? There is a joke among some embroidery circles about changing needles. It goes like this:

(First embroiderer:) How often do you change your needles?

(Second embroiderer:) Every time they break!

This amusing anecdote is reality for many embroiderers. The guideline that many professional embroiderers use is the three strikes rule. Here's how it works. When there have been three consecutive thread breaks on a needle in a relatively short time, the needle should be changed as a simple matter of troubleshooting. This method is used by professionals, because they commonly use multineedle machines and do not track how long a particular needle has been installed.

For a single-needle embroidery machine, you can set up a routine for the frequency of changing needles. Outlines stitch better with a fresh needle, so you may wish to change at the beginning of every project, or after every few hours of stitching. Discard used needles in an old medicine bottle or other sharp-safe container.

It is the simplest thing to check regarding thread breakage, and once removed from the machine, you can check it for burrs or other defects. To test for burrs, run the needle tip across your fingernail or a piece of nylon from a discarded piece of hosiery (fig. 3-8). If it scratches your nail or snags the hosiery, toss it. If you don't detect a burr, place the needle in a medicine bottle with a child-resistant cap. Because you didn't prove it to be defective, you may want to try it again later, perhaps when doing some test sewing. But for the present, go ahead with a new needle to continue with troubleshooting, having eliminated the needle as a possible culprit.

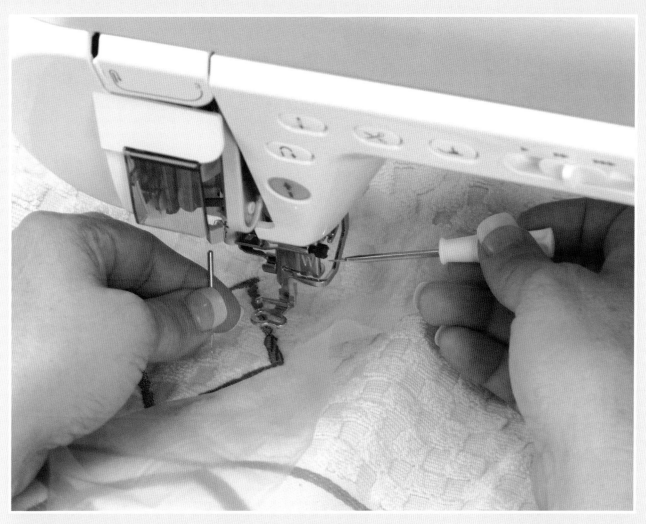

Fig. 3-7. When there have been three consecutive thread breaks on a needle, it should be changed as a simple matter of troubleshooting.

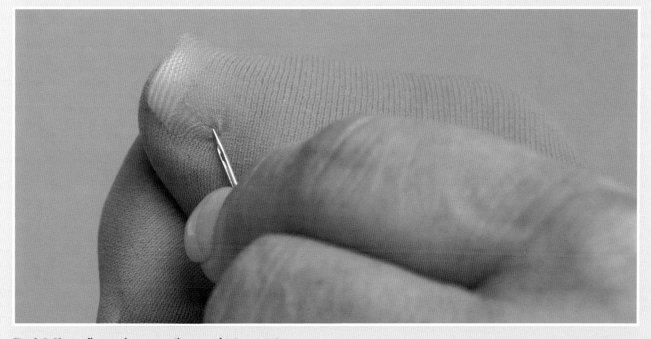

Fig. 3-8. If a needle scratches your nail or snags hosiery, toss it.

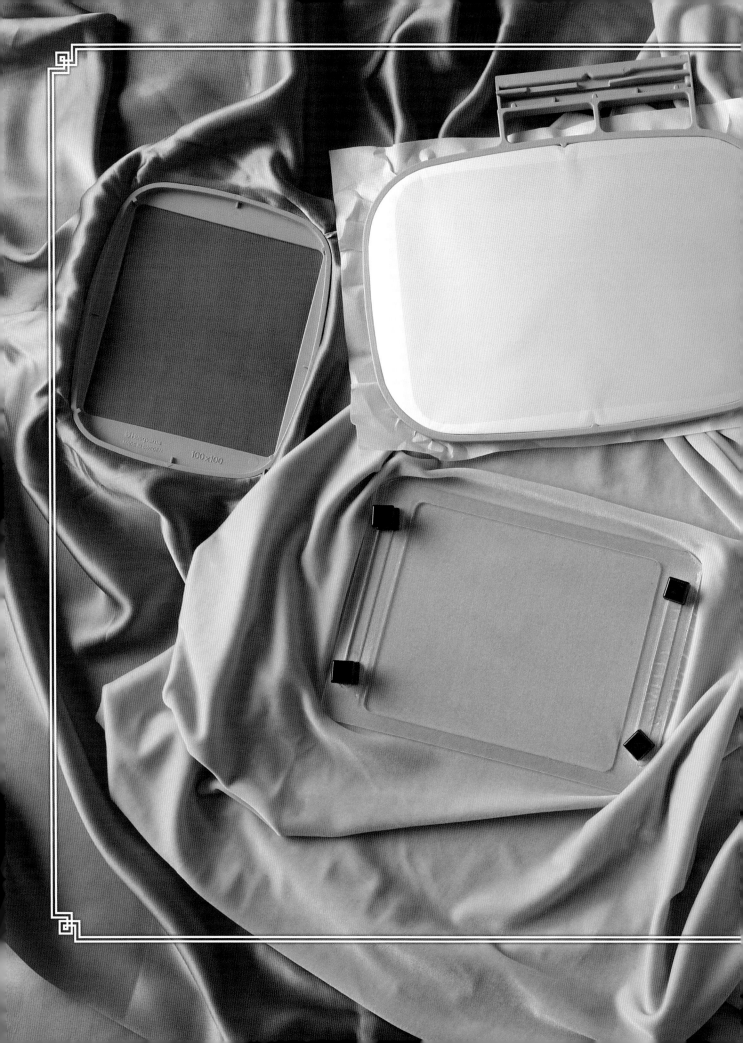

CHAPTER FOUR

Choosing Embroidery Components:

Hooping

For centuries, we have held fabric for embroidery in a two-part hoop. This is still the best way to hold most items for embroidery. When you place fabric in a hoop, you are placing surface tension on the fabric. You must have appropriate tension on your top and bottom threads, and having a light tension on your fabric helps in the embroidery process for many fabrics. Absence of fabric tension may allow puckering and distortion of design elements on unstable backgrounds.

SELECTING THE HOOP

Always choose the smallest hoop that will comfortably accommodate the size of the design. Traditionally, embroidery hoops have been round, because this shape helps spread the fabric equally in all directions. Most hoops available for our home model machines are rectangular, which have their own advantages. It's easy to see when the fabric is straight with the straight edge of the hoop, and they allow a larger embroidery area than a round hoop.

Jumbo hoops and multi-position hoops allow larger embroidery design sizes. The long, flat sides of these oversized hoops may not grip the fabric securely, allowing it to slip during the embroidery process. This can result in puckering or drifting outlines. Get better grip on your fabrics by wrapping the hoop. To do this, wrap the inner ring with fabric, twill tape, or self-adherent tape. These materials provide a gripping surface, rather than slick plastic, next to your fabric. They also protect the fabric from hoop impressions by acting as a cushion (fig. 6-12, page 75).

HOOPING AIDS

A hooping stand (figs. 4-1 and 4-2) will hold the outer ring steady while you apply the inner ring. If you do not use a hooping stand, ask someone who is handy with tools to make a hooping jig for you. A hooping jig is a piece of wood, Masonite, or other material with a cut-out that matches your outer hoop. You will need for the opening to be at least as large as your outer hoop when it is opened to its widest setting. You can insert automotive weather-stripping to the inside of the jig to fill in the gap when the hoop is adjusted for thinner fabrics. Attach the jig to your table to hold the bottom hoop straight while you are hooping.

If you have no hooping stand or hooping jig, you can apply a piece of carpet tape to your hooping table to hold your bottom hoop in position. Carpet tape is sticky on both sides, and you can place it on your hooping table, and place your bottom hoop over it to prevent it from moving while you are hooping.

Cut a piece of your selected stabilizer generously larger than your hoop size. It should be large enough to extend outside your hoop in all directions.

For faster and easier hooping, mark your item for straightness and for the center point of the embroidery. Mark the placement with a long straight line, rather than just a dot, using a disappearing marker, painter's tape, basting tape, or other marking method, making sure that the line is straight with a reference on the item (fig. 4-3). Use a method other than tape when marking napped fabrics or terry cloth so the pile or loops are not pulled when the tape is removed.

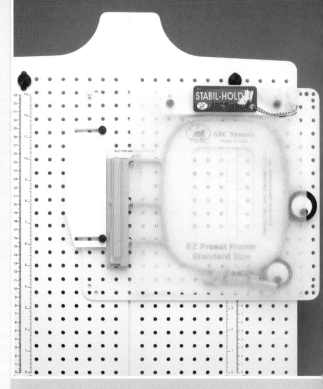

Fig. 4-1. Use a commercial hooping stand or make a jig to hold the outer ring and stabilizer while hooping the fabric.

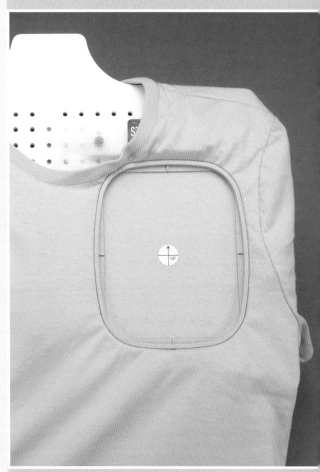

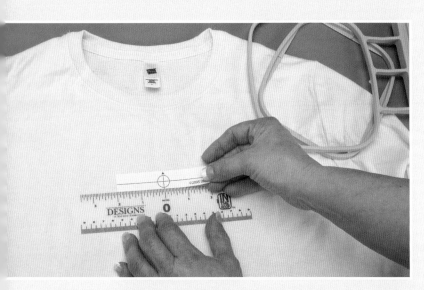

Fig. 4-3. Mark a straight line on the fabric and mark the centerpoint for the embroidery.

Fig. 4-2. A hooping stand leaves both hands free to position and get proper tension on the fabric.

38

This long, straight marking assures that the embroidery will be straight. If the marking appears straight after the hoop has been loaded in the machine, you can feel secure that your embroidery will appear straight.

If you use embroidery software, you may want to print out an image of the embroidery design to pin in position on the item to check more accurately for size and placement (fig. 4-4).

HOOPING TECHNIQUE

Adjust your hoop to accommodate the thickness of the fabric. I tighten the hoop after the fabric has been inserted only on heavy fabrics and leather. If it makes you feel more secure, or if your hoops don't hold very well, go ahead and tighten slightly after hooping. Just remember that over-tightening can bruise the fibers of fine fabrics, and it does nothing to increase the surface tension.

As you begin to insert the inner ring, you should feel moderate resistance. If there is too much resistance, your fabric could be marred. Loosen the screw on the outer hoop ring slightly and try again. Remember, the fabric should be taut, rather than the hoop being tight.

Fig. 4-4. Use templates printed from embroidery software to help assure accurate placement of the centerpoint for the embroidery.

Hooping Checklist

- Select the smallest hoop that will comfortably accommodate the design.

- Mark for straightness and for the center of your design.

- Use a hooping stand, jig, or double-faced tape to hold the bottom hoop ring straight.

- If possible, recess the inner ring to be slightly lower than the outside ring, placing it flat to the machine bed and increasing fabric surface tension.

- Make sure the stabilizer extends from all sides of the hoop.

- Tighten the hoop only slightly, if at all, after hooping, except on very bulky items.

- Try to lift the fabric from the stabilizer layer after hooping. They should be difficult to separate.

- Hoop your stabilizer well enough that you could embroider on it even if the fabric were not present.

When you insert the inner ring, apply the hoop to the fabric at the top or bottom of the hoop, whichever is more comfortable for you. Complete the motion moving continuously toward the other edge of the hoop. You may gently pull the fabric downward while hooping, if you believe it is necessary. This is helpful when hooping knits, but be careful you don't pull too hard, which could result in stretching and distortion of the knit. This can create puckering when the fabric is released from the hoop because the yarn's memory causes it to try to revert to its previous state. The embroidery needle can even burst fibers in the knit if it has been stretched too much in the hooping process, even if it is a ball point needle. While hooping, keep an eye on your marking, making sure that your reference line stays straight with a reference on your hoop (fig. 4-5). Most hoops have notches or other reference points that bisect the hoop. If yours does not, use nail polish or paint to mark the exact center of each of the four sides.

After the fabric is in the hoop, inspect the surface of the fabric. Do you see ripples? If you see a few slight surface ripples, press the inner ring down slightly to remove them. The inner ring will now be slightly lower than the outer ring. Some hoops have a lip that does not allow this. If that is the case with your hoop, you should hoop again and loosen the hoop screw slightly. Frequently, severe rippling is the result of a hoop that is adjusted too tightly (fig. 4-6), forcing the fabric toward the center of the hoop. Do not tug on the fabric to remove severe ripples while the fabric is in the hoop. We all sometimes give a little pull, but try not to get into the habit of routinely pulling out ripples rather than avoiding them through proper hooping.

If your hooped item looks good, try the following tests (see page 47 for photographs). Try to lift the fabric from the stabilizer with your thumb and forefinger. If you can easily lift the fabric (page 47, fig. 5-7), hoop the item again. If it is difficult to separate the two layers, you can move on to the next test, the snowplow test. Run your forefinger across the fabric surface. Does fabric bunch up around your finger (page 47, fig. 5-6)? This is called snowplowing. If you see the fabric snowplow as you slide your finger, rehoop the fabric.

Next, turn the hooped piece over to inspect the stabilizer. It should be flat and smooth, extending from all edges of the hoop (fig. 4-7). Don't be lax on this point, or you will be disappointed in your embroidery result. In fact, your stabilizer should be hooped so well that you could embroider on it even if the fabric weren't present.

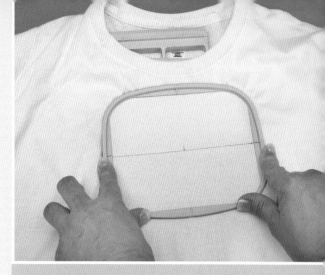

Fig. 4-5. After marking the fabric, hoop it so the line is straight in the hoop. This will assure that the embroidery will be straight.

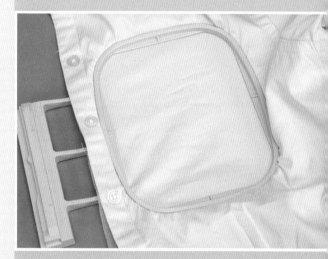

Fig. 4-6. Tightening the hoop too much causes ripples in the hooped fabric.

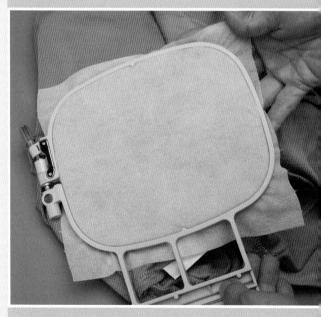

Fig. 4-7. Don't skimp on the size of your stabilizer. It should extend from all hoop edges.

After completing these steps, you are ready to place the hoop in the machine and stitch. After you have removed the item from the hoop, use a damp cloth to remove any hoop ring that shows on your garment. If this doesn't work, moisten the damp cloth with Magic Spray Sizing, available in the ironing-aids department of most grocery and superstores. You can spray it directly from the can onto the garment in the area of the hoop impression, or spray onto a lint-free cloth and dab on the affected area. No ironing is needed.

Adhesive Holding Methods

Many embroiderers use a self-adhesive stabilizer product to avoid the risk of hoop marks. If your design has a lot of stitches or detail, most self-adhesive stabilizers will break down before the embroidery is completed, possibly resulting in misaligned outlines and other problems.

Most self-adhesive stabilizers are very thin and do not offer much support on their own (figs. 4-8A and 4-8B). They can also be difficult to remove from the back of the some fabrics. This is particularly true in the case of textured fabrics. For these reasons, a water-activated adhesive stabilizer, such as HydroStick, is much better suited for certain fabrics than traditional self-adhesive stabilizers. One benefit is that the base stabilizer is much more substantial than most self-adhesive stabilizers. Another benefit is that the adhesive is similar to that on the back of a lick-and-stick postage stamp (remember those?). Just as the adhesive on the stamp is dry once you place it on the envelope, water-activated adhesive stabilizer is dry once you have placed your garment onto its surface. You are not stitching through a sticky adhesive, rather through a dry adhesive that is temporarily bonded to your fabric.

Magnetic Holding System

Some fabrics that are prone to showing hoop marks may be held securely by a magnetic holding system (fig. 4-9). The system has a metal baseplate and clear plastic overlays. The fabric is sandwiched between the metal and the overlay and secured with magnets. I have successfully used the system on such hard-to-hold fabrics as velvet, leather and towels.

To use the system, you still hoop a base of stabilizer that is suited to the fabric. The baseplate is designed to fit inside a standard size hoop for each specific machine brand.

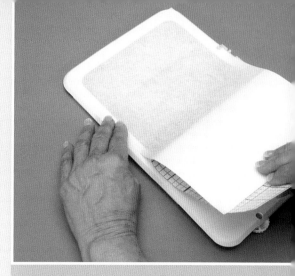

Fig. 4-8A. Peel backing from self-adhesive stabilizer as you apply it to a Hoop-It-All holder.

Fig. 4-8B. Self-adhesive stabilizer applied to Hoop-It-All holder.

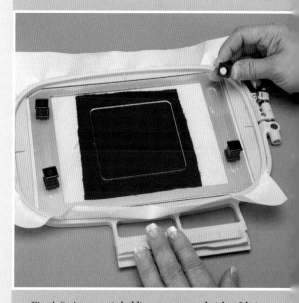

Fig. 4-9. A magnetic holding system sandwiches fabric between a stabilizer base and a Lucite window, using a metal baseplate and magnets.

41

CHAPTER FIVE

Fabrics With

Unstable Backgrounds

Unstable embroidery backgrounds include a range of fabrics that have a tendency to move, stretch, or shift during the embroidery process. This movement and shifting can easily result in design distortion. The more complex the design, the more risk for distortion and misalignment of design elements.

When you think of unstable embroidery backgrounds, what type of fabric leaps to mind? A T-shirt? A sweater? It's natural that many embroiderers relate unstable with knitted fabrics, but some woven fabrics can also be unstable. For example, a lightweight gauze fabric lacks the structure to give it stability of other woven fabrics. Some new broadcloth and poplin fabrics contain spandex for comfort, but this element of stretch can confound the embroidery process. Techniques vary to deal with these different categories of unstable backgrounds, but all can be embroidered successfully.

LIGHTWEIGHT KNIT POLO SHIRT

RECOMMENDATIONS

Needles
Light ball point (HE) Size 70/10 or 75/11
Standard embroidery needles for single-needle home embroidery models have a light ball point, ideal for lightweight knits.

When using standard 40 weight thread, a size 75/11 is suitable. For smaller thread sizes, such as size 60 rayon, the smaller groove and eye of a smaller blade size provide better control, such as a size 65/9. This nonstandard size may not be available in the flat shank version for home embroidery models, and the substitution of a light ball point sewing needle may be necessary. Very lightweight knits, such as so-called tissue weight T-shirts, are knitted from a very fine yarn. A smaller needle size will create less stress on the fabric and give a better result (fig. 5-1).

Thread
My preferred thread types for lightweight knits are rayon or cotton. These natural fibers are not as strong or stiff as polyester, and seem more in keeping with the characteristics of fabrics knitted from fine yarns. Stitches formed from these pliable thread types lay in well, and seem to be a natural part of the garment.

There are good reasons that polyester might be used, such as its resistance to chlorine bleach. So, if your knit project happens to be an infant shirt, polyester could be your best choice.

Stabilizer
Lightweight cut-away PolyMesh or similar variety preferred
Stabilizer is perhaps the most critical element in successful and pleasing embroidery on lightweight knits. It is possible to provide a solid foundation with many types and weights of cut-away stabilizer, but many are incompatible with the goal of maintaining the supple quality of the fabric. Most traditional nonwoven varieties are not suitable because they are too firm. Also, because this type of stabilizer has some degree of stretch, it is usually necessary to hoop two layers at opposing angles to minimize stretch. Two layers, even of a lightweight nonwoven, are too heavy to allow the knit to retain its inherent pliability.

Lightweight Knits

Characteristics
Lightweight knit fabric has slight to moderate stretch. The texture can vary from a waffle pattern found on piqué knit to a very smooth surface. The primary reason that this fabric is used in garment construction is comfort, so it is important that our techniques maintain this characteristic.

Challenges
The main challenge is preventing distortion during embroidery. A secondary challenge is maintaining a supple hand to the fabric. When the fabric is rolled between two hands, there should not be a big difference in the pliability of the embroidered and unembroidered areas of fabric.

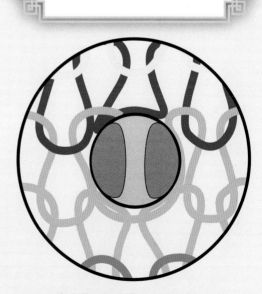

Fig. 5-1. The ball point needle is used with knits because it pushes the knit aside rather than cutting it. This protects its interlocking structure.

It is plausible that a lightweight woven fabric could be a candidate as a stabilizer for this category of knit, although it is not commonly used for this purpose. More commonly used are modern stabilizers created by the spun-bond process (page 24, fig. 2-4). These are very strong, lightweight stabilizers with minimal stretch, making them ideal for this fabric type. Spun-bond stabilizers are available in white, beige, and black, so you can select the most suitable color and virtually eliminate any stabilizer show-through. Spun-bond stabilizers are known under various brand names including PolyMesh and No Show (fig. 5-2).

Spun-bond stabilizer is available in various weights, from about 1 ounce to 1.8 ounces (28 to 51 grams). With experience you will learn which weight is best for a specific project based on fabric weight and stitch count. The most common weight is 1.5 ounces (43 grams). Beginners can feel comfortable about using a single layer of the 1.5-ounce to 1.8-ounce (43g to 51g) weights to provide proper support to their knit projects.

The proper stabilizer is beneficial only if it is hooped properly. In the case of an unstable fabric like a T-shirt knit, all edges of the stabilizer must be secured tautly in the hoop (fig. 5-3). The knit should be smooth and flat on top of the stabilizer without slack that could be pushed by the presser foot.

Fig. 5-2. PolyMesh is a brand of spun-bond stabilizer. It is translucent and has a distinctive waffle-weave texture embossed on its surface.

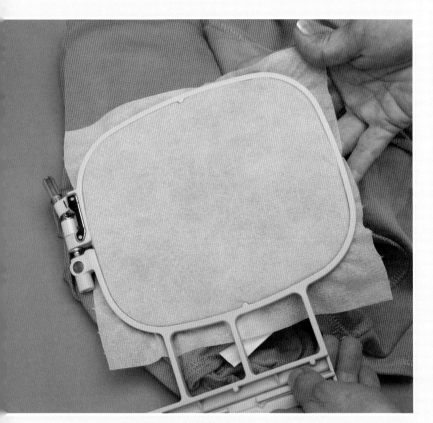

Fig. 5-3. Don't skimp on the size of your stabilizer. It should extend from all hoop edges.

Fig. 5-4. Hoop burn is a term for permanently marred fabric that has been damaged by the hoop.

Hooping

Correct hooping technique is essential for knit fabrics, particularly for detailed multicolor designs, and designs with more than 5,000 stitches. These types of designs should be embroidered only when secured in a traditional two-ring hoop, in the smallest hoop that will comfortably accommodate the embroidery. Even if you have been lucky enough to have successfully embroidered a low-stitch count design using a self-adhesive holding method (also called sticky paper), this method becomes riskier with additional stitch count and detail.

Test for proper fabric tension by running your finger across the hooped knit. It should not snowplow, or create a "bubble," in front of your finger as it travels across the fabric (fig. 5-6). Also, try to lift the fabric from the stabilizer with your thumb and forefinger. They should be difficult to separate (fig. 5-7).

You may tighten the screw on the hoop if you wish, but don't overdo it. Some home hoops have very narrow sides, and tightening may give you an extra bit of security. Be aware that over-tightening can bruise the fibers and result in hoop burn, a permanent hoop impression. Temporary hoop impressions, caused by the hoop being too tight, are common on dark knits, and can be easily removed from any color knit. Purchase a can of Niagara Magic Sizing in the ironing-aids department of any grocery, drug, or superstore. You can spray it directly from the can onto the garment in the area of the hoop impression, or spray it onto a lint-free cloth and dab it on the affected area (fig. 5-5). No ironing is needed.

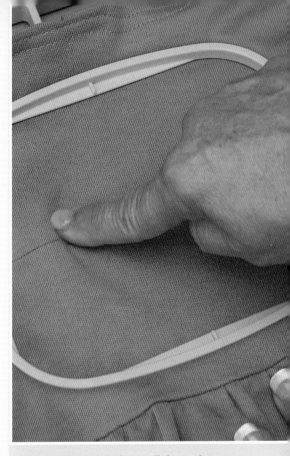

Fig. 5-6. To perform the so-called snowplow test, run your forefinger across the hooped knit, which should remain flat and smooth.

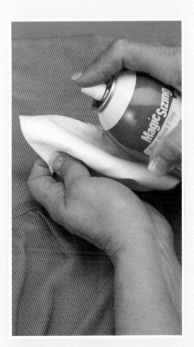

Fig. 5-5. A hoop adjusted too tightly may leave a hoop impression. To remove a hoop impression, apply spray sizing to a lint-free cloth (above, left) and dab it onto the impression (above, right).

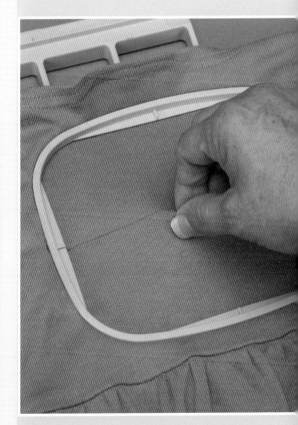

Fig. 5-7. To perform the lift test, try to lift the hooped knit from its stabilizer base. It should be somewhat difficult to separate the two layers.

47

DESIGN PROPERTIES

Density 3.5 to 5.0 (.35 to .5 mm) points
for most satin and fill stitches

Designs with very large fill areas could be heavy and cause soft T-shirt knit to draw inward. Very heavy designs should be avoided when embroidering T-shirt knits. A large fill-stitched area, such as a full chest design, is not comfortable to wear, and it is difficult to embroider effectively without distortion. Rather than embroidering a large area, consider other options, such as appliqué or a heat-applied transfer with embroidered accents (fig 5-8).

If you must embroider a large fill area, you can edit the stitch values to make them friendlier to a lightweight knit fabric. If you are very familiar with embroidery software, lighten the density value and lengthen the fill stitch.

Fig. 5-8. Multimedia methods can help reduce stitch count on lightweight fabrics.

48

An example of a typical density value change is altering the density value from 3.0 points to 4.0 points (0.3mm to 0.4mm). This value measures the distance between the rows of stitches in a fill (fig. 5-9). The measurement is in points; a point equals one-tenth of a millimeter. This change will make each row one-tenth of a millimeter farther apart, resulting in fewer stitches overall.

An example of a typical stitch length value change is altering length of the fill stitch from the typical default value of 3.0 (0.3mm) to 3.8 points (0.38mm) or 4.0 points (0.4mm). This will make the length of each stitch in a fill longer, which results in fewer stitches, and a softer design. When deciding the amount to change this value, consider whether there are design details or lettering that will be stitched on top of the fill area. Make smaller changes, if any, when lettering or fine detail will be applied on top of a fill area.

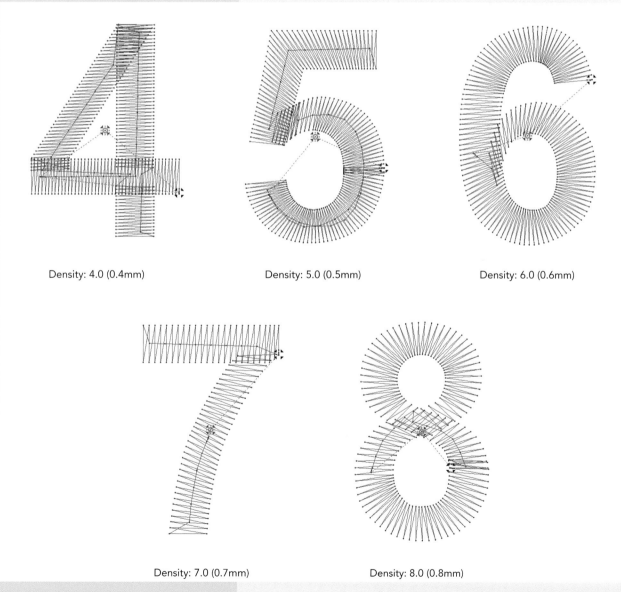

Density: 4.0 (0.4mm)   Density: 5.0 (0.5mm)   Density: 6.0 (0.6mm)

Density: 7.0 (0.7mm)   Density: 8.0 (0.8mm)

Fig. 5-9. Density is simply a measurement of the distance between the stitches. The higher the setting, the greater the distance between stitches.

If you do not have a good comfort level with embroidery software, consider simply enlarging the design without using stitch-processing capabilities. If the stitch count remains the same, but the design occupies a larger area, the rows of fill stitches are placed farther apart, and satin stitches are farther apart. If you enlarge by a value of ten to fifteen percent, the stitches are likely to still be close enough to have good coverage.

Avoid designs with very long satin stitches to avoid design distortion. If you use good hooping technique and appropriate stabilizer, the design may look good when you remove it from your machine. After several washings, however, the design could appear droopy rather than having the same crisp edges along the wide satin columns. If you have a good working knowledge of appropriate software, you could convert the wide satin stitches to fill stitches of a suitable length (fig. 5-10). Some software also has settings for a split column stitch, which divides a wide satin stitch into a blended combination of two meshing satin columns.

Fig. 5-11A. Zigzag underlay is commonly used under satin columns to tack the face fabric to the stabilizer and provide loft.

Fig. 5-11B. Using a double zigzag underlay provides loft and allows a lighter density setting for the final layer of stitches.

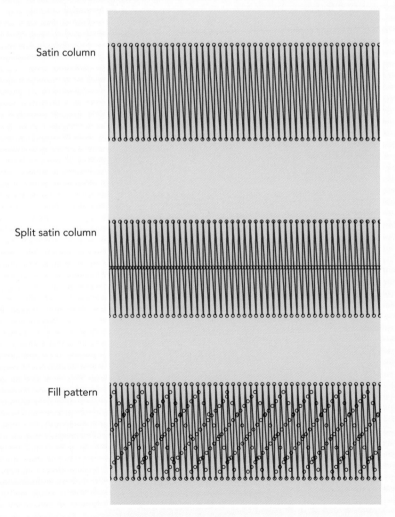

Satin column

Split satin column

Fill pattern

Fig. 5-10. Satin stitches that are too long to be serviceable can be divided into fill stitches or split columns.

Fig. 5-11C. Edge walk under fill stitches should be short enough so they do not pop out from under the fill along curves.

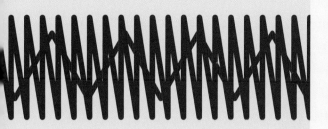

Underlay

Underlay is very important on unstable backgrounds. On these fabrics, it tacks the unstable fabric to the stabilizer, and provides a structured base for the top layer of stitches to grasp onto. Fulfilling both of these purposes may involve two different types of underlay in a single design segment. Let's look at both of these purposes separately.

Under a wide satin stitch, zigzag underlay is typically used to tack the face fabric to the underlay. This is usually the only underlay needed for a smooth knit (figs. 5-11A and 5-11B).

Under a satin stitch that will be applied to a textured knit, such as a piqué or 1 × 1, an underlay type called an edge walk is sometimes coupled with the zigzag. The edge walk consists of running stitches set slightly inside the column that serve as anchors to help hold the edges in place (fig. 5-11C). Also used under fill-stitched areas, these stitches must be fairly short so they do not pop out from under the edges of the top layer of stitches. Because all stitches are straight, when they are too long, there is a tendency for edge walk stitches to protrude from curved edges of embroidery. There are two possible solutions: shorten the stitch length or move it farther away from the edge of the embroidery. This is usually called the inset value.

Different Software Means Different Settings

Various brands of embroidery software use different ways of expressing values for density, stitch lengths, and other measurements. Experiment by noting the stitch count of the design, changing the value slightly and then rechecking the stitch count. In this way you can determine if you are changing the value in the right direction. Always test on a similar fabric before applying an edited design to your project.

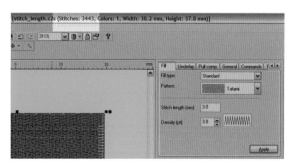

Fig. 5-12. Always check the stitch count before and after applying setting changes to be sure you are adjusting your design in the right direction.

POPLIN-WITH-SPANDEX BLOUSE

RECOMMENDATIONS

Needles

Sharp needle (ST) size 70/10 or 75/11

Flat Shank: Microtex (H-M) or similar acute
round needle in size 70/10

Round Shank: SPI acute round

Despite the spandex content, stretch needles are not called for here. So-called stretch needles are actually heavy ball points (fig. 5-13). This rounded point is intended to push the yarn in a knitted fabric rather than slice through it, damaging the structural integrity of the knit. In the case of this densely woven fabric, a slender sharp point is needed for clean penetration.

Along with a slender tip, a slender blade is also helpful (fig. 5-13). A slender light ball point embroidery needle will work, yet for some designs, a needle made for microfiber sewing may perform better. If you are stitching a fill area, like the one in our example, a microfiber needle will definitely help prevent puckering around the edges of the embroidery. It may sound funny, but when hooped tautly, this fabric is almost like a trampoline, and a ball point needle could almost bounce off, in a figurative sense. A microfiber sewing needle has a point that is even more slender than a regular sharp needle, allowing it to slide easily through this tightly woven fabric.

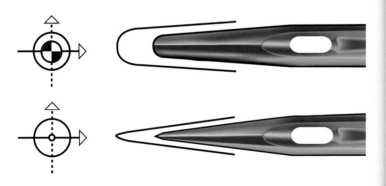

Fig 5-13. A stretch needle, with its heavy ball point (above, top), is made for stitching heavy elastic materials, not lightweight fabrics with spandex content. A sharp, slender needle such as an acute round (above, bottom) will penetrate this type of fabric more cleanly.

Poplin With Spandex

Characteristics

This plain-weave fabric may be woven from cotton and spandex, or cotton/polyester and spandex. The percentage of spandex is low, and the appearance is similar to a typical cotton or cotton/polyester blend poplin. This category of fabric is popular for ladies' blouses and shirts because of the added ease of movement over standard cotton and cotton blends. It is tightly woven, giving it the appearance of a more expensive grade of fabric.Garments made from this type of fabric are commonly sold at retail stores and by large mail order houses.

Challenges

This fabric looks like plain broadcloth or poplin, but it reacts very differently for embroidery purposes. Fill-stitch areas push the fabric out of shape, and outlines may not line up. Before putting an embroidery needle to a woven shirt, check the label to see whether there is any spandex content. The percentage will be low, usually only two or three percent, but that is enough to potentially wreak havoc with your embroidery effort.

Stabilizer

Fusible PolyMesh or similar fusible; light, crisp tear-away 1- to 1.5-ounce (28- to 43-gram)

The best results are achieved on most woven fabrics with a crisp tear-away. Indeed, a tear-away will play a role with this woven fabric as well, but the starring role belongs to a fusible cut-away. The fusible version of nylon spun-bond stabilizer PolyMesh or No Show is one option for the primary stabilizer. ShirtTailor by Pellon, the fusible stabilizer made for garment construction, could also be used. The benefits are that, when fused to the reverse side of this semi-stretch fabric, it prevents stretching both during hooping and embroidery. An additional layer of tear-away can be "floated" beneath the hoop without hooping it in (page 11, fig. 3). This layer of firmer, crisper stabilizer provides more support and resistance to puckering.

Thread

Any high-quality embroidery thread is suitable for use on this fabric. Size 40 or smaller is recommended.

DESIGN PROPERTIES

3.5 to 4.0 points (.35 to .4 mm) for most satin and fill stitches

This fabric should be tested with your specific design before proceeding with the project. Most standard designs with average underlay stitching will work well when the stabilizer guidelines are followed. Because most of the stretch is in one direction, the direction of the fill is important. A fill-stitched area with stitches that run in the same direction of the stretch can cause distortion and push the fabric as it stitches. There are two possible solutions that can be accomplished using embroidery software.

Fig. 5-14. Crosshatch underlay consists of two layers of underlay stitches at opposing angles.

Steps to Stabilize Poplin-With-Spandex Fabric

1. Iron a piece of fusible stabilizer larger than the embroidery hoop on the reverse side of the fabric. If fusible stabilizer is not available, spray a piece of regular mesh stabilizer with spray embroidery adhesive and apply the stabilizer to the reverse side of the fabric in the embroidery area.
2. Hoop the fabric, securing all edges of the stabilizer in the hoop. Place the hoop in the machine.
3. Slide a piece of medium-weight tear-away lightweight crisp 1- to 1.5- ounce (28- to 43-gram) stabilizer between the hoop and machine bed.
4. If puckering or distortion is observed, stop the machine and slide another piece of crisp, lightweight stabilizer beneath the hoop. Restart the machine and observe for puckering. Repeat with another piece of crisp, lightweight tear-away if needed.
5. When embroidery is complete, remove the hoop and tear away the bottom layer of stabilizer.
6. Pull the excess cut-away stabilizer away from the fabric and cut close to the embroidery.

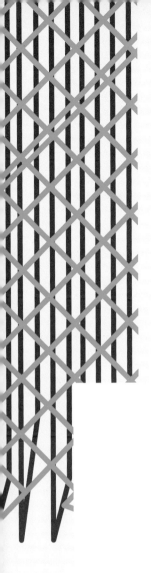

Solution one: Add a crosshatch underlay beneath the fill-stitch area (fig. 5-14). Most underlay stitches run in the opposite direction of the fill stitches that cover it. In a crosshatch fill, the stitches run in two directions.

Solution two: Change the direction of the fill stitch. The direction can be changed to the opposite direction, such as vertical to horizontal, or to a fill that runs diagonally. There are other advantages to a diagonal fill. Knowledgeable digitizers often use diagonal fills where lettering will be applied on top of the fill (fig. 5-15). This is because lettering is composed of many horizontal and vertical elements. Think of the letter T. The crossbar could fall into a vertical direction fill, and the main stem could fall into a horizontal fill. Both would stand up better on a diagonal fill.

Vertical Fill Stitch

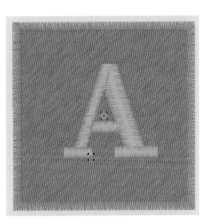

Diagonal Fill Stitch

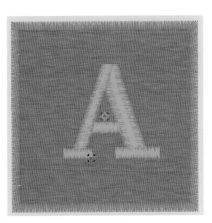

Horizontal Fill Stitch

Fig. 5-15. Diagonal fill is often the best choice when lettering will be applied on top.

MULTIDIRECTIONAL STRETCH KNIT BOTTLE COVER

MULTIDIRECTIONAL STRETCH KNIT

Some garments made of two-way stretch knits, such as neck gaiters, are stretched only when donning the garment, and the knit is relaxed while worn. Others, like swimsuits and bike shorts, are stretched continually when worn. This difference affects the embroidery techniques used for each type of garment.

RECOMMENDATIONS

Needle
Light ball point (H) or medium ball point (H-SUK)
Choose either the light or medium ball point based on the weight of the stretch knit you will embroider. The size of the ball is related to the size of the yarn it is pushing aside when it makes each needle penetration. So, the light ball point is appropriate with lightweight yarns, and a medium ball point will give a better result with heavier stretch knits.

Stabilizer and Hooping
Items that will be relaxed when worn should not be stretched while hooping. To avoid stretching during hooping and embroidery, bond a piece of fusible cut-away stabilizer, such as Fusible PolyMesh, to the back of the knit. This type of stabilizer has minimal stretch and assures that you can hoop without stretching the knit.

Items that will be stretched when worn can also be backed with a PolyMesh stabilizer, but not the fusible variety. In fact, you should pull slightly on the knit while hooping with a lightweight, strong cut-away stabilizer. Applying a slight amount of stretch while hooping will prevent small holes from appearing around the embroidery when the knit is stretched as it's worn.

This may seem odd until you get used to it, and it also makes the finished product look peculiar when not being worn. Because the stretched yarn's memory tries to recover its original position when the garment is unhooped, the displaced fabric bunches around the embroidery area. But when it's stretched over the body, there is sufficient fabric to be stretched without stressing the area around the embroidery (page 16, fig. 1-3B). Hooping a lightweight water-soluble topping in with the fabric will help prevent the presser foot from pushing the knit.

DESIGN PROPERTIES
Density 3.5 to 4.0 point (.35 to .4 mm) for most fill and column stitches
Use moderate underlay to tack face fabric to stabilizer. Slightly widen satin columns to compensate for fabric pull (fig. 5-16).

Multidirectional Stretch Knit

Characteristics
This fabric comes in a variety of weights, from slinky to fairly heavy. The fabric can be stretched in more than one direction, making it popular for active wear. The amount of stretch varies, depending on the amount of stretch fiber in the knit.

Challenges
The stretch is the primary challenge in embroidering this class of fabric, because stretching during embroidery can cause puckering and allow design elements to be misaligned. It is also possible to burst the stretch fibers by using an inappropriate needle type, resulting in damage to the fabric.

Fig. 5-16. *Use moderate underlay and light to moderate density. Slightly widen columns to compensate for fabric pull.*

OPEN BULKY KNIT SWEATER COAT

RECOMMENDATIONS

Needle

Medium ball point (H-SUK)

Bulky knits may be the only time you will embroider with a medium ball point needle. While you could use a regular light ball point embroidery needle, the structure of the knit will be better protected by a medium ball. The heavier point on the medium ball point is more appropriate because the size of the ball point is designed to be relative to the size of the yarn that it is pushing aside as it penetrates the knit.

Fig. 5-17A. Unsuccessful embroidery on bulky knit, which stretches and compresses. The density was too high, compressing the fabric too much. Registration is poor.

Open Bulky Knit

Characteristics

This knit is made from larger, coarser yarn than other knits in this chapter. It may be knitted in a simple repetitive pattern or in a more complex pattern. Bulky knits commonly have "hills and valleys" and are knitted fairly open, rather than tightly, making them very unstable.

Challenges

The main challenges are stretch and difficulty getting good coverage. Another factor is compression, resulting in flat embroidery in the middle of the raised, lofty knit (fig. 5-17A). The open knit allows typical stabilizers to show through.

Fig. 5-17B. Successful embroidery on bulky knit with lighter density (higher point value, fewer stitches).

Stabilizer and Hooping

Standard white or black stabilizer can easily show through a bulky knit. For this reason, the best stabilizer is one that matches the color of the yarn. A very lightweight synthetic fabric in a matching color, such as organza, makes a wonderful stabilizer for bulky or open knits. Free-motion monogram and embroidery artists have favored this reliable stabilizer for decades.

A water-soluble topping should also be used to help create a smooth embroidery surface. Because of the uneven surface, the topping should be a midweight variety, about 35 microns, rather than lightweight. The midweight will not break down as easily, and helps to hold the embroidery on the surface of the knit. The topping should be hooped in with the hoop rather than simply tacking it to the surface of the knit (fig. 5-18). In other words, the hoop will contain a three-layer sandwich. The bottom layer is the organza or similar fabric (fig. 5-19), the top layer is the medium-weight water-soluble stabilizer, and the middle layer is the bulky knit. This is important because the top and bottom layers are stable. When the knit is held inside the other two layers, it is stable during the embroidery process. Tensions should be light to help keep the embroidery from becoming too flat.

Fig. 5-18. With open bulky knits, it is important to hoop the water-soluble topping in with the knit to assure a flat smooth stitching surface.

Fig. 5-19. Stabilize with a matching organza.

DESIGN PROPERTIES

Good underlay structure can help the stitches maintain good loft. A double zigzag underlay works well on satin stitches (fig. 5-20), and a lattice underlay in fill stitches provides a good base (fig. 5-21). Columns should be of sufficient width to stand out against the bold architecture of the knit. Increase the column width using column width or pull compensation settings in your embroidery software (fig. 5-22). Stitches can be a bit longer than standard in fill areas to help create more loft. Unlike some of the other fabric types in this chapter, a bulky knit benefits from application of embroidery at standard density values. The default values of 3.0 points (0.3mm) to 4.0 points (0.4mm) for satin and fill stitches should provide good coverage when combined with appropriate underlay.

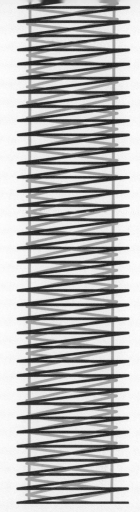

Fig. 5-20. Double zigzag with edge walk allows use of a very light density on the top layer of stitches.

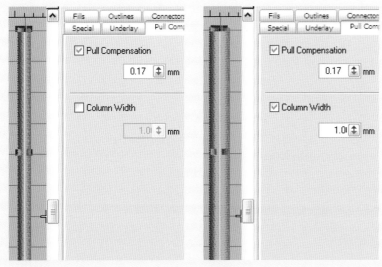

Fig. 5-22. With objects selected, use Column Width or Pull Compensation settings to make satin objects bolder.

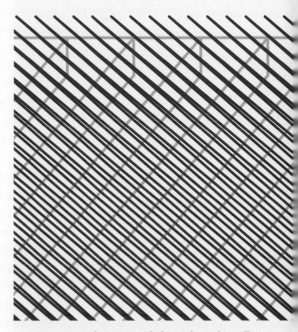

Fig. 5-21. Light tatami underlay with an edge walk will provide good support and clarity to fill-stitch areas.

61

GAUZE SWIM COVER-UP

RECOMMENDATIONS

Needle
Sharp needle (ST) size 70/10 or 75/11

Stabilizer and Hooping
You can give more body to this type of gauze using liquid stabilizers. Some manufacturers have products that you can spray or brush onto the fabric to stiffen it for embroidery. Starch can also be used, but remember that the fabric must be capable of supporting the embroidery after any type of liquid stabilizer has been removed. Liquid stabilizer is usually removed by washing the fabric following embroidery. With any liquid stabilizer, you may also need to use a tear-away stabilizer beneath the fabric.

You can make you own liquid stabilizer with scraps of leftover water-soluble stabilizer. Dissolve the equivalent of about one yard (one meter) of regular or midweight water-soluble topping in 8 ounces (225ml) of water. If you plan to store your solution for an extended period, add a small amount of rubbing alcohol to prevent mold forming. Apply the solution with a brush. This type of stabilizer is most suitable for simple decorative stitch designs.

One of my favorite stabilizers for use with gauze fabric is a midweight or heavyweight water-soluble stabilizer. It is suitable for light to medium stitch count designs. You can hoop in a layer of water-soluble stabilizer beneath the gauze and add a layer of lightweight water soluble on top for best clarity. High stitch count designs may require a traditional tear-away stabilizer beneath the fabric. Using a water-soluble stabilizer has the advantage that it does not show through the lightweight fabric and can be easily and completely removed by washing the fabric.

If you want to use a midweight or heavyweight water-soluble stabilizer, you can buy one such as Super Solvy or Ultra Solvy. You can also make one from regular weight water-soluble topping. Here's how: Place three layers of regular weight stabilizer between two layers of plain brown Kraft paper, such as a grocery bag. Press the layers together until they are fused, using your household iron on a low heat setting (fig. 5-23).

DESIGN PROPERTIES
This fabric has a surface texture that may need to be controlled, depending on how much crinkled effect the fabric has. Light underlay is helpful to make the embroidery stand above the crinkled surface. Like some of the other fabrics in this category, densities on the lighter end of the scale will give a more pleasing result. Fills and satin stitch density should be in the range of 3.5 to 4.0 points (0.35mm to 0.4mm).

Gauze

Characteristics
Gauze used for garment construction is an open-weave fabric made with lightweight to midweight yarn. The breathability of this fabric makes it popular for casual wear including blouses, dresses, and swimsuit cover-ups. It may have a crinkled appearance.

Challenges
Gauze is perhaps the most unstable of woven fabrics because of its open weave. It doesn't have a lot of body, and this makes it difficult to stabilize for embroidery.

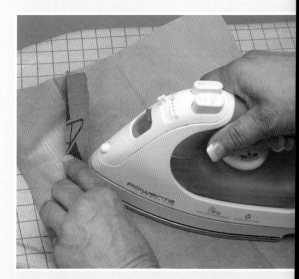

Fig. 5-23. To make your own midweight stabilizer, press three layers of regular weight stabilizer between layers of brown paper bag until they are fused, using your household iron on a low heat setting.

CHAPTER SIX

Densely Woven Fabrics

Woven fabrics usually embroider well, with predictable results. They are stable, and most require only a layer of lightweight stabilizer for a good result on a wide variety of design types.

It can be a shock when such a seemingly friendly fabric type presents problems. Suddenly, a whole range of symptoms may appear. You may experience looped stitches, skipped stitches, puckering, or even see the formation of thread balls under the fabric, commonly called bird's nests. In this chapter we will look at the challenges associated with several densely woven fabric types and solutions for predictable embroidery results.

LIGHTWEIGHT NYLON LADIES' RAINCOAT

RECOMMENDATIONS

Needle

Sharp needle size 70/10 or 75/11

Microtex or similar acute sharp needle in size 70/10

Because of its tendency to pucker, use a needle that slips easily through this tightly woven fabric. The two main factors that affect ease of needle penetration are blade size and point type. A slender blade has less surface area to contact the fabric, resulting in less friction. It's important to select a blade that is slender enough to slip through the fabric easily, but not so slender that it can be deflected by a tough fabric (fig. 6-1).

Similarly, friction is reduced with a more slender point. Most embroidery needles have a light ball point. A light ball point needle appears to have a sharp point, but it is actually slightly rounded. This slightly rounded point is ideal for embroidering knitted fabrics because it gently pushes the yarn aside (fig. 6-2). A light ball point may also be used successfully on some woven fabrics, but it's easier for the more slender point of a sharp point needle to penetrate densely woven fabrics.

There are sharp points and even more slender points called acute sharp points (fig. 6-4). You may have used acute sharp point needles for sewing microfiber fabrics. Even though they are technically designed for sewing rather than for embroidering, it is acceptable to use an acute sharp needle for embroidering dense, lightweight woven fabrics.

You may not be able to find a sharp point embroidery needle at your local store, because standard embroidery needles have a light ball, or universal, point. They are available from suppliers in our Resources list (page 123).

Fig. 6-1. A point and blade size that are correct for the fabric will help avoid needle deflection on a tough synthetic fabric.

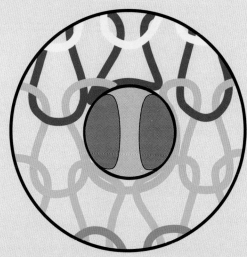

Fig. 6-2. The light ball point was designed for pushing aside the yarns in a knitted fabric.

Lightweight Nylon

Characteristics

This type of lightweight nylon is frequently used for its water resistant properties. It is used in camping gear and windbreakers. It typically has a plain weave and a high thread count. "High thread count" means that it is tightly woven.

Challenges

Tightly woven lightweight fabrics often pucker when sewn or embroidered (fig. 6-3). Puckering is readily apparent when sewing a seam, but it may not be as apparent when the fabric is held taut in an embroidery hoop. Unfortunately, the severity of the puckering may become obvious only after the embroidery is complete and the hoop is removed.

With this fabric type, puckering can result from one or more of the following: inappropriate type or amount of stabilizer, inappropriate needle point type, poor hooping technique, and/or stitch density that is too heavy.

Stabilizer

Medium weight 1.5- to 2-ounce (43- to 57-gram) crisp tear-away, hooped in with fabric

A crisp tear-away (fig. 6-5) will provide the body needed for this fabric to properly support embroidery. Multiple layers may be used depending on the size and stitch count of the design. If multiple layers are used, remove them one at a time to avoid stressing the stitches.

If you detect puckering around the edges of the embroidery while stitching, stop the machine and slide an additional piece of crisp stabilizer between the hoop and machine bed. Stitch a bit more and repeat if needed. This technique is known as "floating" stabilizer, because it is not held in the hoop. It is not generally preferred as the primary stabilizing method, but can be useful for adding stabilizer as needed.

Hooping

Nylon fabric can show hooping marks that may be difficult to remove. To reduce this possibility, remove the hoop as soon as embroidery is complete. To buffer the hard plastic of the hoop against the nylon, wrap the hoop or use a buffer layer between the inner hoop and the fabric.

The hoop can be wrapped with self-adherent tape, which is designed to cling only to itself (fig. 6-7). This safe wrapping material can be purchased at drugstores and will leave no residue on your fabric or hoop.

In addition to reducing the tendency of nylon to show hoop marks, the tape wrapping also provides grip on the slippery nylon. This is particularly helpful on high-stitch count designs, because each needle penetration can loosen the hoop's grip. For best holding, hooping in a traditional two part hoop is preferred for best results on this fabric type.

Fig. 6-3. Improper needle use, too many stitches or improper hooping technique can all result in puckering on dense synthetic fabrics.

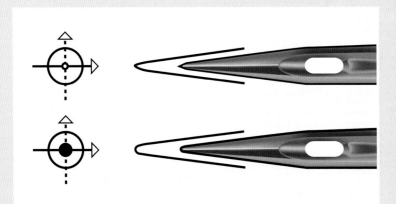

Fig. 6-4. The slender sharp point of the acute round (Microtex) needle (above, top) is able to penetrate tightly woven fabrics cleanly. The commonly used light ball point (above, bottom) does not penetrate as easily and could result in puckering.

Fig. 6-5. A crisp multidirectional tear-away tears in much the same way as paper. It tears as cleanly in one direction as another.

68

Thread
Rayon or Polyester, size 40

DESIGN PROPERTIES
Density
3.5 to 4 points (.35 to .4 mm) for most satin and fill stitches
This will place slightly fewer stitches in the fabric than a typical default density value of 3 points. Good coverage can be achieved with this moderate setting, and any tendency to puckering will be diminished.

Underlay
Zigzag for satin stitch areas, approximately
   20 points (2.0 mm) density
Light tatami for fill-stitch areas
Underlay serves different purposes for different fabrics, and with this fabric type, it serves to attach the stabilizer to the face fabric (fig. 6-6). For this purpose, the amount of underlay stitches can be minimal. They should cover the entire surface of the design, rather than just a walk stitch around the perimeter. Applying underlay stitching throughout the design creates a base that will help eliminate pushing of this lightweight fabric. If pushed, it can become trapped and pleated by subsequent embroidery.

Fig. 6-6. A 20 point-underlay serves to attach stabilizer to fabric face.

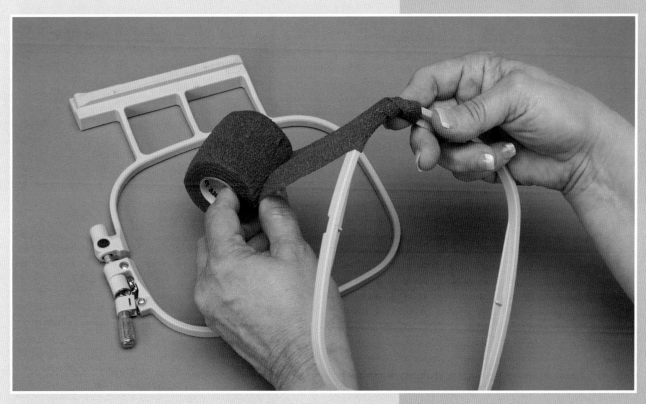

Fig. 6-7. Self-adherent tape wrap on hoop reduces marks and fabric and helps increase grip for nylon ripstop.

CORDURA NYLON GIRLS' BACKPACK

RECOMMENDATIONS

Needles
90/14 Embroidery needle, 90/14 Jeans needle

Stabilizer
Medium weight 1.5- to 2-ounce (43- to 57-gram) crisp tear-away, single layer

This fabric is very stable even without stabilizer. The stabilizer helps assure that the fabric glides easily across the machine bed.

Thread
Polyester thread may be needed to keep thread breakage under control.

Hooping
Two-part hoop or self-adhesive stabilizer

This stiff fabric can be difficult to hold in a two-part hoop, particularly if the item is bulky or must be hooped near seams. Experiment with hoop direction until the item lies as flat as possible, then turn the direction of the design in the machine accordingly. In some cases, best results are achieved using a self-adhesive stabilizer either hooped in a two-part hoop or attached to a fixture such as a Hoop-It-All (fig. 6-8). Hoop the self-adhesive stabilizer with the release paper facing up, and score the paper to remove it from the embroidery area only.

DESIGN PROPERTIES

Density
4.0 points (0.4mm) for satin stitches and fill stitches

Underlay
Minimal
Zigzag for satin stitch areas, about 20 points (2.0mm) density
Light density tatami for fill-stitch areas

Underlay stitching can help to attach this fabric to a carrier of self-adhesive stabilizer, providing a more secure hold.

Cordura Nylon

Characteristics
This coarse nylon fabric is highly resistant to wear. It is suitable for items that will be subjected to sunlight, water and abrasion.

Challenge
This stiff fabric is hard to hold. The coarseness of the nylon may cause thread breaks when using natural thread such as rayon. The coarse weave may cause jagged edges on small lettering and column stitching (fig. 6-9).

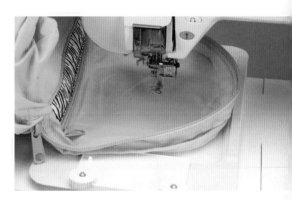

Fig. 6-8. Hoop self-adhesive stabilizer with the release paper facing up, and score paper to remove only in the embroidery area.

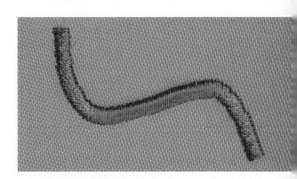

Fig. 6-9. Although a stable fabric, the coarse weave can result in jagged edges on small columns. Very small letters under 3.8 inches (9.6 cm) and fine detail should be avoided.

71

POLYESTER SATIN AND ACETATE SATIN DOG PILLOW

Photo © Steve Woods, Elevate Group, Dallas, Texas

RECOMMENDATIONS

Needle
70/10 Universal or light ball point embroidery needle

If you are an experienced seamstress, you possibly use a sharp point needle for seaming satin fabric. However, embroidering delicate satin fabric with a sharp point can cause excessive cutting of the fabric because of the closer proximity of embroidery stitches.

It is also important to change the needle frequently because the slightest burr on the needle can cause the fabric to "run" similar to runs in nylon hosiery. Examine the fabric surface frequently during embroidery for symptoms of puckering or running.

Stabilizer
Light to Medium weight 1 to 2 ounces (28 to 57 grams) crisp tear-away, single or multiple layers, hooped in with fabric

Hooping
Traditional two-part hoop; avoid self-adhesive stabilizers

The delicate surface of satin can be easily marred by a rough spot on a hoop. Protect the surface of satin, and get better grip, by applying a piece of tissue paper over the area to be hooped, with the dull side facing the fabric. Apply the top hoop over the tissue paper. After hooping, tear a window in the tissue paper to accommodate the embroidery (fig. 6-11). The tissue paper is a quick and easy alternative to wrapping your hoop. You may use a hoop wrapped in self-adherent tape; however, you should make sure that the tape has not been exposed to heat, which can make the tape tacky.

Thread
Rayon size 40, polyester size 40

Rayon is most compatible; this natural fiber lays well into the fabric and has similar softness and sheen. Polyester may also be used.

DESIGN PROPERTIES (FIG. 6-10)

Density
3.5 to 5 point (.35 to .5 mm) density on satin stitch and fill stitches

Underlay
Minimal

Zigzag for satin stitch areas, approximately 20 points (2.0 mm) density

Light density tatami for fill-stitch areas

More underlay may be used to add loft to satin stitches if desired.

Polyester and Acetate Satin

Characteristics
In a satin weave, the warp threads cross over three or more backing threads, so that the warp threads float on the surface, creating a lustrous and reflective finish on the front and a dull finish on the back.

Challenges
Puckering, running, marring and slippage in hoop can occur.

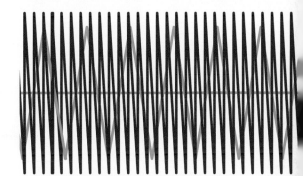

Fig. 6-10. This example is 0.4 point satin density with 20 point underlay.

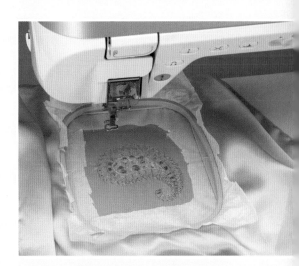

Fig. 6-11. Regular tissue wrapping paper can help prevent fabric slippage while also protecting delicate satin from rough spots on the hoop. Hoop dull side down.

SILK CHARMEUSE SCARF

Silk

RECOMMENDATIONS

Needle
Sharp needle size 70/10 or 75/11
Microtex or similar acute sharp needle in size 70/10

Stabilizer
*Light to midweight 1 to 2 ounce (28 to 57 gram) crisp tear-
    away, single or multiple layers, hooped in with fabric*

Hooping
Traditional two-part hoop. Avoid self-adhesive stabilizers which
may be difficult to remove, reducing the supple hand of the fabric. A
wrapped hoop can help prevent fabric slippage (fig. 6-12).

Thread
Rayon size 40, polyester size 40
Rayon is the most compatible because this natural fiber lays well
into the fabric and has a similar softness and sheen. Polyester may
also be used.

Consider using more open areas in your designs to allow the
beauty of this natural fiber to show through. Use a light tension
setting on your thread, and consider using a natural fiber thread
such as rayon or cotton, depending on the finish and desired effect.

DESIGN PROPERTIES
3.5 to 5 point (.35 to .5 mm) density on satin stitch and fill stitches

Underlay
Minimal
*Zigzag for satin stitch areas, approximately
    20 points (2.0 mm) density*
Light density tatami for fill-stitch areas
More underlay may be used to add height to satin stitches if desired.

Characteristics
Silk is a strong natural fiber, woven
into a wide range of fabrics. These
fabrics may be crisp or supple,
sheer or substantial. Synthetic
fibers are tough, but natural fiber
silk can be equally challenging
to embroider. An interesting
testament to the strength and
toughness of silk is that early
Mongol warriors wore a silk
garment under their armor to stop
arrows from deeply penetrating
the body. The arrow could be
popped out by pulling on two
sides of the silk.

Challenges
Puckering and hoop slippage.

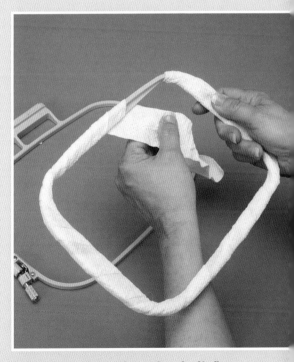

Fig. 6-12. *Wrap the inner hoop only with self-adherent
tape to provide better grip on the fabric without leaving
a residue.*

75

CHAPTER SEVEN

Pile and Napped Fabrics

If you have ever had your beautiful design swallowed up by the deep pile of a fabric, you will never forget the feeling. It looked so beautiful on the screen. Perhaps you even took some steps to help keep it atop the mounds of fiber. Many of us have had thoughts of just pressing the start button again, completely restitching the design a second time, on top of the original. I have even done the second layer at times, especially on lettering. The result may have been a bit dimensional but it certainly didn't look skimpy!

Through experience I have learned ways to avoid my designs being lost on plush fabrics. Starting with manipulating the design at the computer, through using toppings at the machine, and sometimes, special finishing techniques, I have become more successful at embroidering on these fabrics. This chapter has many insights to help your embroidery stand out on deeply textured fabrics.

VELVET COSMETICS BAG

RECOMMENDATIONS

Needle
Sharp or light ball point embroidery needle

Stabilizer
Use one or more layers of lightweight or midweight crisp tear-away beneath the fabric. The amount needed will be determined in part by the holding method you select. When the velvet is held more securely, less stabilizer is required.

With any pile fabric, toppings provide a smooth, flat embroidery surface and hold the pile in check during stitching. Water-soluble and heat-dissolving toppings must be used with care on velvet. While heat-dissolving topping may work with some types of velvet, it is not compatible with acetate, and pressing velvet tends to crush it. It is also inadvisable with velvet to use permanent plastic or vinyl toppings; such toppings could react with dry-cleaning solvents, becoming stiff or even damaging the fabric.

The best way to use water-soluble topping on velvet is to tear it away after underlay stitching is completed and before the final layer of stitching is applied (figs. 7-3A–7-3C). A light- or midweight water-soluble topping is ideal.

Velvet

Characteristics
Velvet is a woven fabric with a pile surface, usually made from rayon, cotton, acetate, or polyester. It has a lush appearance, and the surface feels soft, while the base beneath may be somewhat crisp.

Challenges
There are several challenges in embroidering velvet; indeed, there are challenges even in handling it. Velvet creases easily, and standard means of holding velvet for embroidery can leave marks. Some velvet is sensitive to water, meaning water-soluble toppings cannot be used in the manner usually employed with napped fabrics. The pile of velvet is very upright (fig. 7-1) and may lie down in any direction when contacted by the presser foot, making velvet more difficult to control than napped fabrics that lie in one direction. Detailed or high-stitch-count designs can cause velvet to pucker (fig. 7-2).

Fig. 7-1. Velvet pile peeks through embroidery thread when no topping is used.

Fig. 7-2. Detailed or high-stitch-count designs on velvet must be held securely or the velvet will crawl and pucker, as in this sample (seen from the wrong side).

79

Existing designs may require editing in embroidery software to add underlay or to force the underlay stitching for each color to be executed in its entirety before the final layer is applied.

Hooping

Holding velvet without crushing or marking it is perhaps the most challenging aspect of embroidering it successfully. Nontraditional holding systems such as magnetic frames and certain clamps can work very well. Traditional two-ring hoops can also be used with some modification in technique. The outer ring should be wrapped with a non-sticky, self-adherent tape to serve as a cushion against the velvet. Then open the outer ring as wide as possible. The gripping properties of the self-adherent tape will usually hold the velvet without detectable marks, so long as the velvet is removed promptly following embroidery.

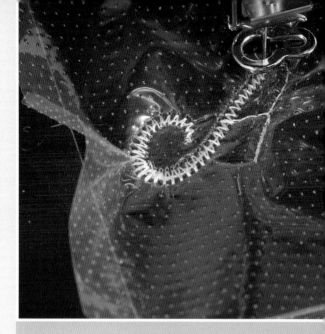

Self-adhesive stabilizer, otherwise known as "sticky paper," is not generally suitable for a fine fabric like velvet because it can be difficult to remove completely. It could be used for designs without small openings and for items where complete removal is not necessary.

Some embroiderers secure velvet by spraying a stabilizer with embroidery spray adhesive, hooping the stabilizer and finger-pressing the velvet onto the surface of the hooped stabilizer. This method may work, but as with pressure-sensitive stabilizer, it may be difficult to remove the stabilizer completely.

Another way to hold velvet is with a magnetic holding fixture (fig. 7-3C). The Magna-Hoop is an accessory that works with your regular embroidery hoop and is available for most machine brands. The first step is to hoop a base of stabilizer in your standard hoop, which is topped by a metal baseplate with a large opening. There are several clear plastic overlays with various size openings, so that you can match the size of your embroidery to the smallest opening that will accommodate the embroidery. The clear plastic overlays are backed with rubber strips that grip the surface of the velvet and help to control its tendency to creep. Small openings in the overlays allow furnished magnets to be inserted to further secure the fabric.

Creeping velvet can also be controlled with the use of basting stitches. Some machines have a basting or fixing stitch feature that applies a basting stitch outside of the selected embroidery design. If your machine does not have such a feature, you can digitize rectangles of various sizes to serve the same purpose, or use hand-applied basting stitches.

Fig. 7-3A. Apply clear topping and stitch underlay through the topping.

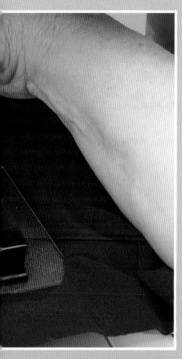

Fig. 7-3B. Tear away the topping after the underlay stitching is complete.

Fig. 7-3C. Stitch final layer after topping has been removed for a clean finish.

Thread

Any thread type can be used on velvet. Metallic thread is even more beautiful on this rich canvas than perhaps on any other. Polyester can be used, but cotton and rayon are not as stiff as polyester and lay in more softly.

DESIGN PROPERTIES

Simplicity of design is best with velvet because it is not held in the hoop as firmly as other fabrics. To help understand the design challenges associated with velvet, let's think of a simple star design. The wide stitches in each arm of the star require more density because wider satin stitches need more density to achieve good coverage. Now think of the points of the star. The small points at the tips of each arm are buried in the velvet. Topping and underlay can help the wide stitches achieve proper coverage and to help the narrow points have clarity.

Free-motion embroiderers frequently "trace" the elements with light coverage in one direction, and then repeat one or more times before applying the final layer. This technique builds up the stitching to rich, raised, lush embroidery. Because the velvet foundation fabric is also lush, this technique creates a particularly appealing appearance on velvet. The effect can be re-created in digitized designs by repeating underlay stitching layers, making them slightly wider with each pass. Making each layer slightly wider avoids placing too many needle penetrations in exactly the same location, stressing the fine fabric and possibly causing thread breakage.

TERRY CLOTH TOWEL AND ROBE

RECOMMENDATIONS

Needle
Light ball point embroidery needle or sharp point needle

Stabilizer
One layer of midweight tear-away is usually sufficient for hooped terry. Unfortunately, some home machine hoops will not open wide enough to hold a thick towel and many embroiders just find towels too difficult to hoop. It's tempting to use self-adhesive stabilizer as a base to hold towels, but the sticky stabilizer can pull the terry's loops when the towel is removed from the adhesive base.

There is a solution that involves the use of a second stabilizer, a fusible one. Water-soluble or other topping is also needed to create a smooth stitching surface. A water-soluble topping may give a false sense of security on terry because after it has dissolved, the loops are free to work themselves up through the stitching if they have not been sufficiently anchored with underlay stitches. For large monograms, you can use more permanent toppings such as dry cleaning bags, clear kitchen wrap, vinyl, or even lightweight tear-away stabilizer.

Any of these permanent toppings will never be dissolved through washing, and the terry loops will not work their way through your monogram even after years of laundering. A thin vinyl topping product called Dry Cover-Up is available in colors to match your stitching. To use any of these more permanent top-pings, follow this sequence: Stitch the underlay, stop the machine, tear away the topping and resume stitching (pages 80–81, figs. 7-3A–7-3C).

Terry Cloth

Characteristics
Terry cloth comes in looped and sheared varieties, referred to as velour. There are many grades of quality in terry cloth, and inexpensive grades are somewhat open and unstable. For the purposes of embroidery, terry cloth and velour terry are fairly predictable embroidery surfaces.

Challenges
The loops or pile of terry cloth can obscure embroidery details and bury small design elements. Loops and pile can also peek through the embroidery unless special preventive measures are used. Lint and loose threads can leave debris in machine parts.

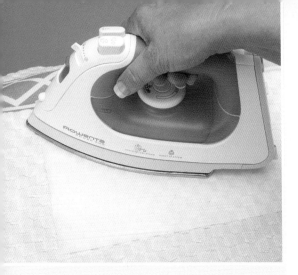

Fig. 7-4A. Adhere light-tack stabilizer to embroidery area on reverse side of towel.

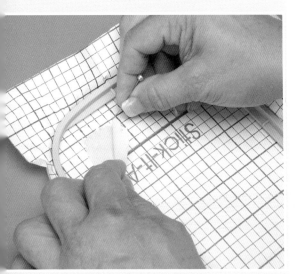

Fig. 7-4B. Prepare hoop with self adhesive stabilizer.

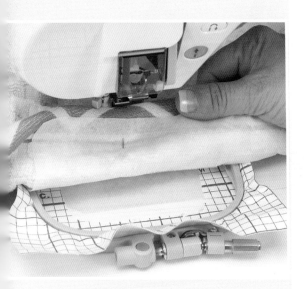

Fig. 7-4C. Place towel with backing into the machine over the hoop that has self-adhesive stabilizer in it.

Hooping

As mentioned in the stabilizer section, applying bare terry to a self-adhesive stabilizer causes pulled loops on the back of the fabric when it is removed from the base. To solve this, there must be a buffer layer between the terry and the adhesive (fig. 7-4C). Interestingly enough, the best buffer is a fusible tear-away stabilizer with a light tack. Two products of this type are Totally Stable by Sulky and FaBond by Hoop-It-All. Just iron lightly to the reverse side of the terry, covering the area that will be adhered (fig. 7-4A). Following embroidery, lift the terry from the stabilizer and gently pull away the fusible stabilizer.

It may seem strange to use a fusible stabilizer to protect the loops from the adhesive, but when lightly fused, the fusible tear-away can be removed from the towel with no loop damage at all (figs. 7-6A and 7-6B). Terry embroidered using this method has no hoop marks to be removed and there is no adhesive stabilizer to dig out of crevices in the embroidery.

If you choose to insert terry cloth into a hoop, then hoop it together with a layer of tear-away stabilizer underneath. Lightly rub the hoop impression with a damp cloth after removal and the loops will spring back into place.

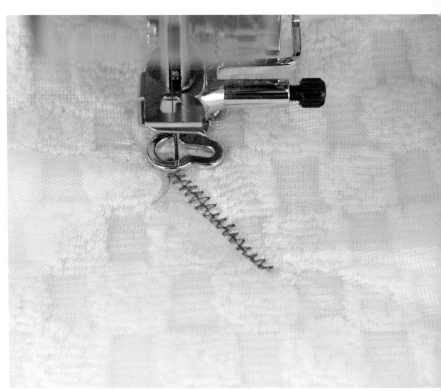

Fig. 7.5. Zigzag underlay helps control pile and give embroidery a rich, raised appearance.

DESIGN PROPERTIES

As mentioned, even with permanent or temporary topping, it is necessary to use underlay stitching in designs used on terry cloth (fig. 7-5). You may choose to space your underlay stitches more closely than usual to help give the top layer of stitches more loft. Some commercial embroiderers use what virtually amounts to two layers of stitching at a standard density value to create monograms that are deep and rich. This is possible because high-quality terry cloth will stand up to this amount of stitching. While the result is pleasing for simple monograms, it is very time-consuming and possibly not a good idea for home machines. A better approach is to use a double zigzag underlay at a density value of 10 points (1.0mm) rather than a more typical underlay value of 20 points (2.0mm) (fig. 7-7).

Eliminate unnecessary detail, or choose simple designs with bold elements for best results. You may need to widen columns so that they stand out against the loops or pile. Do this using the "Pull Compensation" feature of your embroidery software, starting with a 10 percent or 15 percent increase and working up from there as needed.

For fill-stitched areas, use a cross-hatch underlay at a standard value, combined with a mask. While it is pleasing for satin stitched areas to look lush, it is not pleasing for a fill-stitched area to look bulky. It's also possible, if not likely, that lettering or details might be applied on top of the fill, so you don't want a thick base that could prevent clean needle penetration.

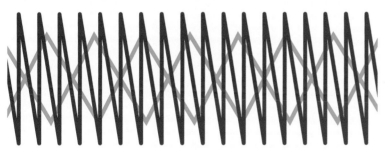

Fig. 7-7. Home machines can achieve a professional look using a double zigzag underlay combined with a final layer at 3.0 point (0.3 mm) density.

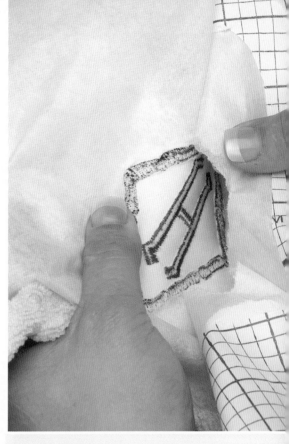

Fig. 7-6A. Pull towel from stabilizer base.

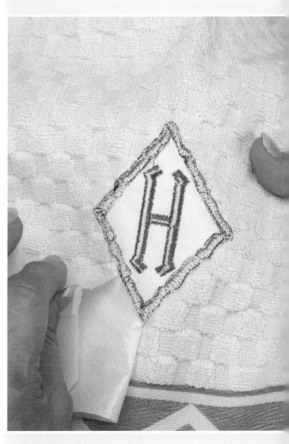

Fig. 7-6B. As Totally Stable is removed, no loops are pulled.

Welcome♥
AnneMarie
May 8, 2008

FLEECE LAMB

RECOMMENDATIONS

Needle
Light ball point embroidery needle

Stabilizer
Soft tear-away or PolyMesh type cut-away

Your choice between the recommended stabilizers, soft tear-away or polymesh cut-away, will depend in part on the number of stitches in your design and its complexity. Small, simple, one or two color designs will embroider well with a good quality soft tear away (figs. 7-11 and 7-12). Designs with more stitches and more detail will be better supported by cut-away.

Regardless of which stabilizer you select, hoop it in completely with the fleece. Don't be fooled by the substantial appearance of polar fleece—it's a knitted fabric and is subject to shifting.

Hooping
As we mentioned, polar fleece is a knit, so you need to control shifting of the base and the pile. A two-ring traditional hoop, MagnaHoop or other method that secures or sandwiches the fabric is best. You can adhere fleece to a self-adhesive base if the stitch count is low and there isn't a lot of detail or outlining. Minimize hoop impressions by using a moderate tension setting on the hoop.

DESIGN PROPERTIES

The guidelines for fleece are similar to those for towels. One additional tactic that some professional embroiderers use on fleece and similar pile fabrics is to lay down a base of light density fill stitches in the same color as the fleece. Lettering or other embroidery is applied over the base of light density fill stitches rather than directly to the pile. In this case, heavy underlay is not needed because the pile is flattened by the light density fill. The shape of the fill may be a rectangle, oval, or sculpted to the shape of the lettering or design elements.

The density value for the fill-stitch area should place the stitches very far apart. Remember that density values measure the distance between the stitches, so to program a very light density for a fill area, enter a density value of 20 or even 30 points (2.0 or 3.0mm). If you don't digitize, but can edit, just edit a fill shape from a design in your library as your base to flatten the pile. Open the design and delete all the elements except the fill. Select the fill area and change its properties. Then merge your lettering or other embroidery over the fill.

Fleece

Characteristics
This fabric is knitted from polyester yarn in a variety of weights and densities, with a surface that has been brushed with wire brushes and then sheared to various pile heights. It can have a variety of surface effects from Berber to plush, but the most common type encountered by embroiderers has an even pile height.

Challenges
The main challenges are preventing embroidery from sinking into the deep pile and maintaining proper registration of design elements. One of the main differences between this fabric and many other pile fabrics is that it is knitted rather than woven, making it less stable.

Fig. 7-11. Soft tear-away (above, left) looks fuzzy along the edges because it is made of both short and long fibers. Crisp tear-away (above, right) tears more like paper.

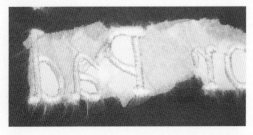

Fig. 7-12. Note the long fibers in this soft tear-away.

FAUX FUR WINE COZY

RECOMMENDATIONS

Needle
Light ball point 75/11

Stabilizer
Midweight tear-away

Hooping
Because of the thickness of faux fur, it may not be possible to hold in a two-ring hoop. It's fine to adhere faux fur to self-adhesive stabilizer for embroidery, but you must stay near the machine to make sure that it remains in place throughout the process. If the fur is particularly hard to keep in place, hoop a piece of cut-away stabilizer and baste the fur fabric top to it.

DESIGN PROPERTIES
The design must be bold, with any satin stitches wide enough to stand out against the fur. Underlay must be generous (fig. 7-13). For satin stitches, use a double zigzag, and for fill stitches use a cross-hatch underlay. The final layer should be a density of 3.0 points (0.3 mm) for good coverage.

After removing the topping, you may see that the pile creeps on top of the edges of the embroidery. There are a couple of ways you remove the excess pile to showcase the embroidery. The first is similar to giving the fur a haircut. Using sharp, short blade scissors, trim the longer fibers in the embroidery area. A quicker and more natural look can be achieved by using an electric trimmer. I use a Peggy's Stitch Eraser, which is a tool marketed primarily for removing embroidery stitches. Holding this trimmer upside down, at a slight angle, you can gently sculpt the fur surrounding the embroidery area (figs. 7-14A and 7-14B). Certain personal trimmers will work for this purpose as well.

Faux Fur

Characteristics
This fabric is woven or knitted and has tufts of fiber forming a pile surface. The fiber encountered by embroiderers is often acrylic, but other fibers are also used.

Challenges
The main challenge is the unusual length of pile as compared to fleece, velvet, and other pile fabrics. Even when embroidery is applied using a topping, the pile can easily obscure the embroidery after the topping is removed.

Fig. 7-14A. Without trimming, the letters are hard to see.

Fig. 7-14B. Hold the tool at an angle for a smooth cut with a natural appearance.

Fig. 7-13. An effective way to embroider faux fur is to lay down a base of light-density underlay.

89

CHAPTER EIGHT

Leather and Imitation Leather

Leather is one of the richest canvases for the embroidery stitch. Regardless of what you may have heard, garment leather is friendly to the embroidery process. Most embroidery horror stories regarding leather are most likely based on embroidering on leather that is unsuitable. In this chapter you will learn how to identify leather that was intended for garments and leather that was processed for other uses, such as tooling embossed patterns.

Some of my earliest embroidery experiences were based on leather embroidery, because my father was fascinated with creating successful leather embroidery. As a well-known Western tailor, leather seemed to go hand-in-glove with his embellished western apparel. Lose your fear of leather and you will gain many rewarding embroidery experiences.

LEATHER LADIES' BOMBER JACKET

Leather

Characteristics

Garment leather has a smooth side, called top-grain, and a textured, side called suede. Frequently, either side is usable for garment construction or embroidery.

Split suede has been split to a desired thickness and has a suede surface on both sides. This leather can be used for garments or embroidery, although it is weaker than top-grain leather. Deer skin, sheep skin and goat skin are other sources of lightweight leather suitable for garment construction.

In natural leather there is a wide range of weight and thickness. Thin leather may be soft and supple or hard and brittle. A major influencing factor is the tanning method. Certain leather that has been tanned using vegetable or oak tanning methods may not be suitable for embroidery. These hard leathers are too stiff for embroidery, but they hold their shape well and are ideal for tooling. Thick or thin, this leather tends to perforate when penetrated repeatedly by an embroidery needle.

Most garment leather is chrome tanned using chromium salts, resulting in soft pliable leather that is easy to embroider. Leather weight is defined in ounces, which used to be based on the weight of one square foot of the leather. Today the system has been simplified so that each ounce is equal to about 1/64 inch (0.4mm) of thickness. Generally, leather up to about 4 ounces, about the thickness of a quarter, can be embroidered on a home machine depending on other characteristics such as softness and pliability.

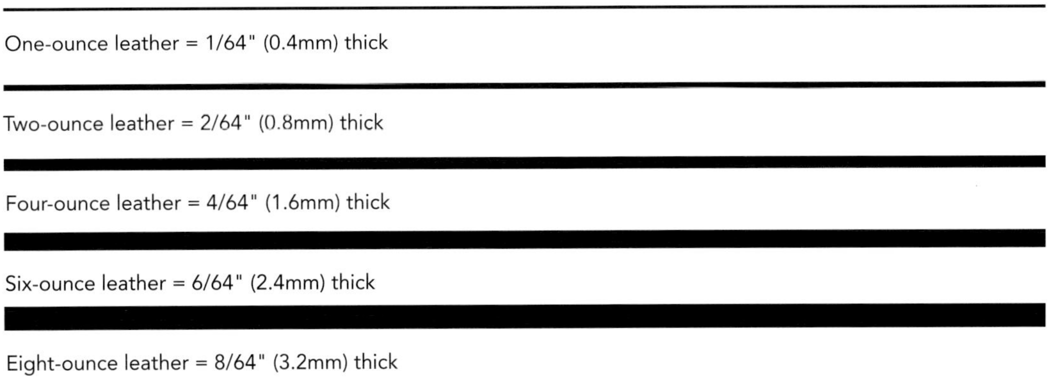

One-ounce leather = 1/64" (0.4mm) thick

Two-ounce leather = 2/64" (0.8mm) thick

Four-ounce leather = 4/64" (1.6mm) thick

Six-ounce leather = 6/64" (2.4mm) thick

Eight-ounce leather = 8/64" (3.2mm) thick

Fig. 8-1. Soft garment leather up to about four-ounce weight can be successfully embroidered on a home machine.

Challenges

Many embroiderers won't attempt to embroider on leather, but the truth is that it's pretty fun. My father specialized in embroidering on leather, and I guess that I was just never afraid of it. One of the main reasons that embroiderers are reluctant to embroider leather is that once a hole has been placed in leather, it's there to stay. That fact alone is enough to scare many embroiderers away from working with leather. In addition, leather has a natural tendency to stretch and perforate and the potential to show hoop marks.

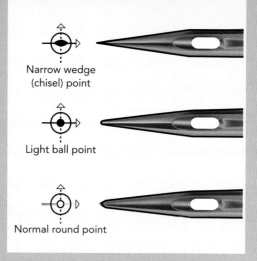

RECOMMENDATIONS
Needle
Light ball point or normal round (sharp) point

When sewing a seam in leather, the proper needle is a wedge or chisel point. These needles have a specially designed cutting point to help make straighter seams than conventional needles. However, because these needles make a large hole, they are not well suited to the close proximity of needle penetrations resulting from embroidery.

There is a type of wedge-point needle with a narrower point that many people believe is appropriate for embroidery applications because it makes a smaller hole than the standard wedge point. Based on my experience, I prefer to use either a normal round (sharp) needle or a ball point needle. This is partly because the cutting points of these needles slice the leather, and the color of the top grain does not always match the color of the inside of the leather. The wedge-point needle can expose the inside of the leather along the edges of the stitching.

My general rule for selecting a needle for soft leather is to begin stitching with a normal round (sharp) needle, because this point type makes the smallest hole. If I notice that the leather is being lifted on the needle's upstroke, I switch to a light ball point. The light ball point makes a slightly larger hole, which will usually allow the needle and thread room to escape on the needle's exit, or upstroke.

The ball point is also a good choice for hard or spongy leather. Many of the thread breaks experienced during leather embroidery are caused by friction that is created when the leather closes up around the needle and thread. If the point type does not provide a large enough hole for the needle and thread to exit easily, try the next larger size blade with a light ball point (fig. 8.2).

Fig. 8-2. Cutting needles, such as the Narrow Wedge Point (top), were designed to help make straight seams. They should not be used for embroidery because of the close proximity of embroidery stitches. The Wedge Point's hole size (indicated by the shape inside the circle at top left) and sharp edges can damage the material or previously applied embroidery stitches. Notice the large, long hole created by the Narrow Wedge Point versus the smaller holes created by the Light Ball and the Normal Round.

Stabilizer

Hydro-Stick or similar, ShirtTailor by Pellon,
medium to heavy cut-away

You should always use some type of stabilizer when you embroider unlined leather, even if the leather seems substantial. Among other benefits, the stabilizer helps to keep debris from the leather out of the hook assembly area of your machine. When you can access the back of the leather, such as is possible on unlined leather items, the very best stabilizer is one that can be adhered to the back of the leather.

Even though leather is sensitive to both water and heat, with care you can use a water-activated or heat-activated adherent stabilizer. ShirtTailor by Pellon is available at most fabric stores, and it has a very low melt point, making it suitable for use on the reverse side of leather. Cut a piece larger than the hoop, and carefully iron it on the embroidery target area using a household iron on low heat.

When the back of the leather is accessible, another good stabilizer choice is Hydro-Stick, or a similar stabilizer with a water-activated adhesive. I find the water-activated to be a better choice than self-adhesive stabilizers on leather. Self-adhesive stabilizers have a tendency to grab the needle and thread, and coupled with leather's tendency to do this, the combination can result in unnecessary thread breaks.

The benefit of water-activated adhesive stabilizers, unlike self-adhesive stabilizer, is that the adhesive is dry when it is stitched. This makes it much friendlier, and the grip is more than adequate if properly applied. Rather than using a sponge to moisten the stabilizer as some recommend, I prefer to use a moistened paper towel. A slightly damp paper towel doesn't deposit as much water and is easier for me to control than a sponge (fig. 8-3).

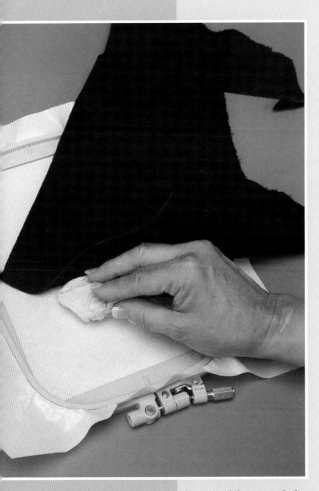

Fig. 8-3. Water-activated adhesive stabilizers are ideal for leather because they are dry, not sticky, when stitched. Moisten it with a damp paper towel.

Upon completion of the embroidery, any adherent stabilizer may be difficult to remove because the textured suede side of the leather provides excellent grip. It can always be removed, but you may not always want to.

When you don't have an adherent stabilizer for use with bare leather, a medium weight or heavyweight cut-away stabilizer will work well and prevent stretching. When embroidering lined leather, the lining acts as a stabilizer. You can reinforce the stabilizer effect of the lining by adding one or two pieces of tear-away stabilizer. If the garment has a dark lining fabric, use a black tear-away for aesthetic reasons.

Hooping

Most high-quality top-grain leather can be hooped without leaving marks. The main thing to remember is to never force a hoop onto leather. If you use a traditional two-ring hoop, consider wrapping the inner ring with self-adherent tape (fig. 8-4). This tape sticks only to itself and will not leave a residue on the leather. It provides a cushion for the leather, reducing the risk of marking the delicate, smooth surface of top-grain leather. You can purchase it in a drug store or pet supply store. Look for names such as NexCare, Pet Wrap, and Vet Wrap. It also allows you to use a light setting on the hoop screw and still keep the leather held securely.

Leather is one exception to my general practices for hooping. I normally try to preset the tension on my hoop to be appropriate for the fabric before applying the hoop. With leather, apply a slightly looser hoop and tighten slightly after the leather is in the hoop to avoid marring the leather.

Nontraditional holding methods such as the MagnaHoop are an excellent alternative. The MagnaHoop holds leather securely without leaving marks. The gripping strips make good contact with the texture of leather and prevent slipping.

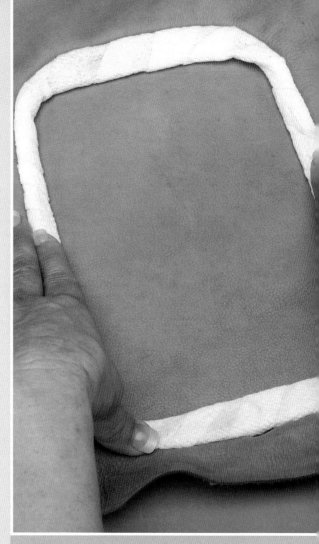

Fig. 8-4. A wrapped hoop allows the hoop tension to be set more loosely and still provide good grip and avoid marring of the leather.

DESIGN PROPERTIES

Choose simple designs when you are embroidering your first leather projects. When possible, reduce the detail in highly detailed designs (figs. 8-5A and 8-5B). For example, if you have a horse design with outlined hooves, remove the outline on the hooves. The design will still look great, and you will reduce the chance of misaligned embroidery.

Most garment leather will not "punch out" when embroidered. That is only a risk with leather that has been made for tooling rather than embroidery. You don't need to drastically reduce your needle penetrations for leather. A density of 3.5 to 4.0 points (0.35 to 0.4 mm) on fills and satin stitched areas should work well. Even 3.0 points (0.3 mm) may be appropriate on certain designs and leather types—you don't want to push the leather out of shape or stress the leather.

It can also be pleasing to let the leather show through in fill-stitched areas (fig. 8-6). Leather is a beautiful natural canvas for embroidery. This is one reason why it is advisable to test your design on leather before stitching it on your project. You can buy test scraps of leather from leather suppliers in our Resources list (page 123) or just pay a visit to your local thrift store and purchase inexpensive leather garments for testing purposes. They are well worth the small investment.

Fig. 8-5A. Original design without adjustments for leather.

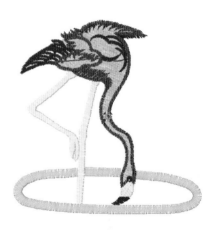

Fig. 8-5B. Certain outlines and other small details have been removed, resulting in a design better suited to leather. Outlines that are off-track cannot be invisibly removed from leather.

Fig. 8-6. Although normal densities will work on garment leather, allowing some leather to show through the embroidery adds appeal and is less stressful to the leather.

FAUX SUEDE ALBUM COVER

RECOMMENDATIONS

Needle
Light ball point or MicroTex (fig. 8-7)
Most faux suede stitches beautifully using a standard light ball point embroidery needle. If you experience stitching problems such as skipped or loopy stitches, be prepared for a bit of experimentation. Different manufacturers use different manufacturing methods, so your faux suede may react better with a larger needle size, or even a Microtex needle made for microfiber fabrics.

Stabilizer
Adherent stabilizer or soft tear-away
My favorite stabilizer for faux suede is Hydro-Stick. It has the right amount of body and eliminates stretch. A soft tear-away also can provide good support even on a heavy design. Soft tear-away has more resistance to perforation than crisp tear-away and this makes it a good base for materials that have some natural body of their own.

Faux Suede

Characteristics
Faux suede is lightweight and more supple than natural suede. It is a nonwoven microfiber material that can be washed or dry-cleaned. Trademarked UltraSuede comes in various weights suited to their use, such as upholstery or fashion.

Challenges
The fashion weights of faux suede are lightweight and can be stretched during embroidery. The delicate surface can also be imprinted by the presser foot of the embroidery machine.

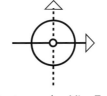

Acute round or MicroTex

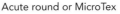

Light ball point

Fig. 8-7. A light ball point or acute round (MicroTex) point are the most suitable needle types for faux suede. The type used will depend on the weight and characteristics of the specific faux suede.

Hooping

If you hoop faux suede, remove it from the hoop promptly. Do not pull on faux suede because you can stretch or tear it. I prefer to hoop HydroStick and apply the faux suede to it. The key to working with a water-activated stabilizer is using the correct amount of water to activate the adhesive properties (fig. 8-8). Too much water can activate too much adhesive for your specific material, causing it to be difficult to remove without wetting. You can also diminish the holding properties with extreme over-wetting of the adhesive. Sponges can apply too much water, so I use a moistened paper towel to dampen the surface of the stabilizer slightly. Then I finger-press my faux suede piece onto the stabilizer base.

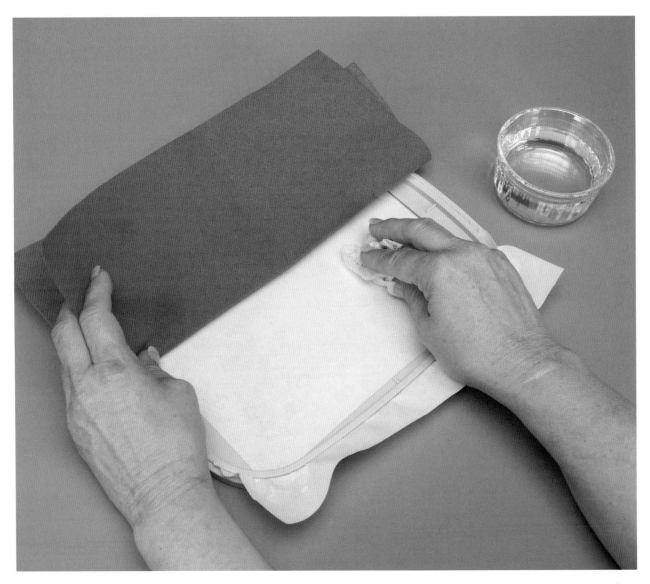

Fig. 8-8. Water-activated stabilizer is ideal for holding faux suede and minimizing stretch. To avoid over-wetting the stabilizer, dampen the stabilizer surface with a moistened paper towel.

DESIGN PROPERTIES

Use moderate density settings with standard underlay settings (fig. 8-9). It isn't necessary to use extreme editing methods for faux suede, because it is quite user friendly for embroidery. Most designs that stitch successfully on a woven fabric will also stitch well on faux suede. As with leather, be careful not to put any unneeded holes in faux suede because they cannot be removed. Like leather, it can be pleasing to let some of the rich faux suede surface show through the embroidery.

Bags of scraps of faux suede can be purchased from sources in our Resources list (page 123). They are inexpensive and are great for practice.

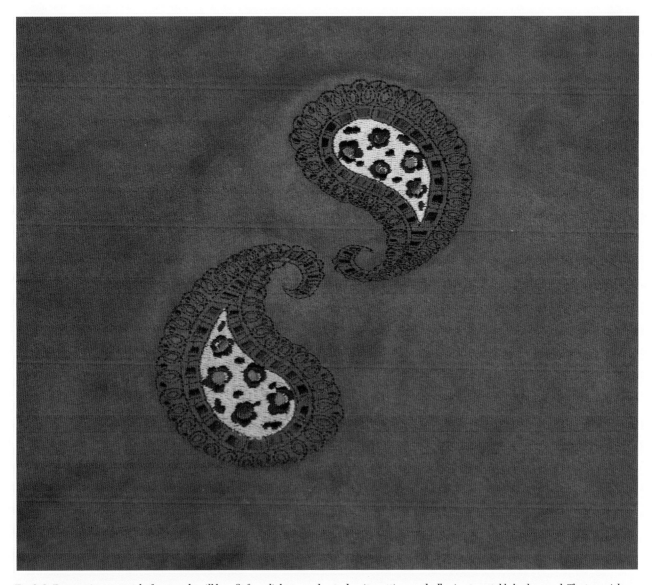

Fig. 8-9. *Because it can stretch, faux suede will benefit from light to moderate density settings and adhering to a stable background. The top paisley has too much density and has stretched the suede.*

VINYL TOTE BAG

RECOMMENDATIONS

Needle

Small-blade sharp needle
You can, and should, use a smaller needle blade on vinyl than on leather. Use a sharp needle point to make the smallest possible hole.

Stabilizer

Because of vinyl's tendency to stretch, try to use a stabilizer that can be adhered to the reverse side of the vinyl. Heat-fusible stabilizers are not an option for use with vinyl because it is very heat sensitive. Water-activated adhesive stabilizers are excellent for use with vinyl. Before they existed, I used the old-style water-activated shipping tape with good success. You can also adhere a standard stabilizer with embroidery spray adhesive.

Hooping

Vinyl is very susceptible to hoop impressions. If you must hoop it, leave it in the hoop only as long as absolutely necessary. It's better to use a nonstressful method, such as an adhesive stabilizer, a magnetic hoop, or a clamp.

DESIGN PROPERTIES

Vinyl designs should have light density with minimal underlay. Laying in too many stitches in vinyl could cut or stretch it. Unlike fabrics, where too many stitches in a concentrated area cause it to draw in and pucker, too many stitches in vinyl can cause the embroidered area to stretch and pooch (fig. 8.10). A light underlay will help tack the vinyl to the stabilizer, minimizing the stretch.

Use a light density setting, such as a 4.0 or 5.0 points (0.4 to 0.5mm) on satin stitched outlines to prevent cutting, particularly on vinyl that does not have a bonded backing of its own (fig. 8-11).

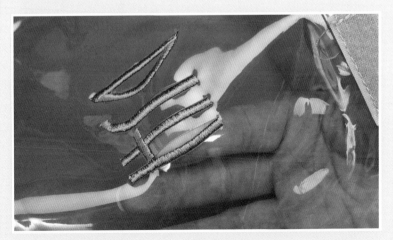

Fig. 8-10. Too many stitches will not only cut vinyl, but may also make it stretch or pooch.

Vinyl

Characteristics

Vinyl may have a smooth or textured surface, and frequently has a bonded backing of some kind. It is very durable, water-resistant, and used for embroidery purposes. We see vinyl in functional items such as handbags and utility items. It is sometimes used as a substitute for leather and has the benefit of having a uniform weight. It is heat sensitive.

Challenges

Vinyl stretches and perforates. Both of these characteristics must be controlled for successful embroidery. Even though embroiderers are perhaps more apprehensive about embroidering leather, vinyl can be equally challenging.

Fig. 8-11. Evaluate a test stitching to determine the lightest density that will achieve the desired coverage.

103

CHAPTER NINE

Sheer Fabrics

Sheer fabrics are a delight—their wispy ways are enchanting, particularly with the added interest created by expertly applied embroidery. Our enchantment may turn to dismay if attempts to embroider are foiled by puckering, stabilizer show-through or other disappointing results. From traditional heirloom embroidery on sheer cotton organza to elegant all-over motifs on synthetic sheers, embroidery seems magical on these fabrics, as it should. It should seem as though it simply appeared there.

With just a bit of practice, you can master these lighter-than-air materials. In this chapter, you'll find the key to keeping the inherent qualities of the fabric after applying decorative embroidery.

NATURAL-FIBER SHEER RING BEARER'S PILLOW

RECOMMENDATIONS

Needle
Sharp, size 70/10
A small sharp needle should be used to prevent the appearance of needle holes at the edges of the embroidery. It will also diminish any saw-tooth appearance of satin stitches.

Stabilizer
Generally, with "see-through" fabric, your stabilizer should be transparent, particularly if your design has lots of nooks and crannies where bits of stabilizer will remain. A traditional non-woven stabilizer, no matter how lightweight, will show through your fabric (fig. 9-1). You could spend hours picking out stabilizer, risking fabric pulls or other damage.

Instead, use water-soluble stabilizers with sheer fabrics (fig. 9-2). There are many weights of water-soluble stabilizer available. I use a midweight product such as Super Solvy. Ultra-heavyweight water-soluble stabilizers like Romeo or Ultra Solvy are too heavy if you intend to remove the stabilizer by tearing it away as I do.

Heat-removable clear-film stabilizers are also an option. Tearing away a heavy stabilizer can distort the fabric or the stitching, or both. Heavyweight water-soluble could be used if you intend to soak the fabric to remove it. This is would be possible with synthetic sheer cotton, but it would not be desirable with sheer silk and rayon fabrics that should not be wetted with water.

Natural-Fiber Sheers

Characteristics
Sheer natural fibers are very charming when embroidered. The combination of sheer natural fabrics and embroidery evoke feelings of nostalgia even when the embroidery has been created by machine. The sheer cotton fabric in our handkerchief project is somewhat crisp because it is impregnated with sizing. Once laundered, it will be much softer and somewhat limp unless starched. Sheer natural fabrics that are soft or crisp can be embroidered with the methods described here.

Challenges
Sheer natural fabrics have a tendency to allow show-through of the stabilizer. Untrimmed threads also show through if not removed. These lightweight fabrics frequently pucker when embroidery is applied.

Fig. 9-1. When small openings, such as those in lettering, are present, a nonwoven stabilizer is not well suited on sheers because of show-through.

Fig. 9-2. Even when not removed completely, transparent water-soluble stabilizer does not show through sheers.

If testing shows that you need more support than a single layer of midweight water-soluble provides, consider using two layers of medium weight water-soluble. When removing the stabilizer, I gently tear it away, leaving minimal bits of transparent remnants. The appearance and drape of your fabric will not be affected. If your design is very solid, without a lot places where stabilizer can hide, you can test the suitability of a crisp tear-away (fig. 9-3).

The tear-away should be very crisp—one that tears away easily after being penetrated by the needle. After embroidery, the fabric should still feel supple when rolled between your hands where the embroidery is applied.

Fig. 9-3. When a design is solid, nonwoven stabilizers may be used for excellent support without show-through.

Hooping

Sheer fabrics should be hooped in a hoop or holding fixture rather than using any type of adhesive holding method. Hoop the fabric entirely in the hoop, and hoop the stabilizer entirely in the hoop. Use the smallest hoop that will accommodate the embroidery design.

If your hoops have any burrs or rough spots, avoid snagging the fabric by wrapping the hoop (page 96, fig. 8-4) with twill tape or a self-adherent wrap such as VetWrap, Pet Wrap, or a human version sold at the drug or grocery store. A wrapped hoop also provides a better grip on sheer fabrics.

Alternately, hoop a layer of tissue, matte side down, between the fabric and the inner ring of the hoop (fig. 9-4). Tear a window in the tissue that is large enough for the embroidery in the area where the embroidery will be applied. The tissue provides a buffer layer between the hoop and the fabric and is an acceptable alternative to wrapping the hoop.

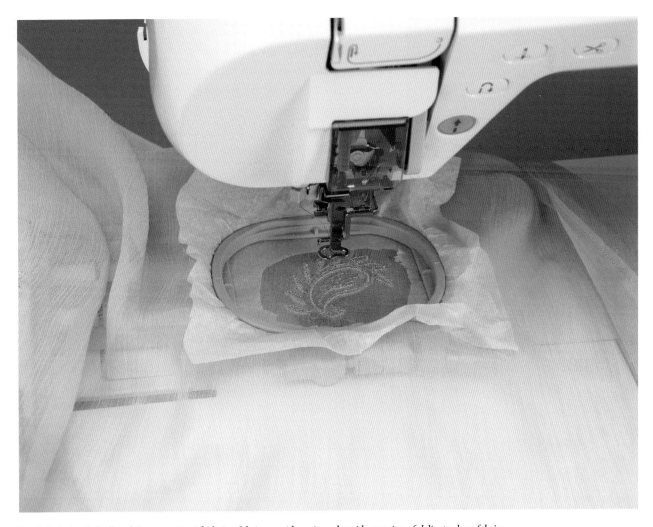

Fig. 9-4. A simple buffer of tissue, matte side facing fabric, provides grip and avoids marring of delicate sheer fabrics.

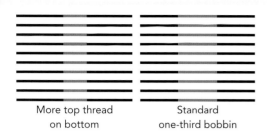

More top thread on bottom   Standard one-third bobbin

Fig. 9-5. Loosen the top tension, allowing more top thread to flow to the back of the fabric, to create less stress on delicate sheer fabrics.

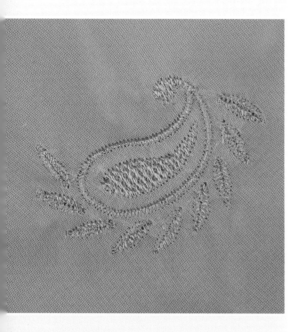

Fig. 9-6. Carefully trim away all excess thread tails from the reverse side because they are visible through a sheer fabric.

Thread

Rayon or cotton embroidery threads are the best choices for embroidery on sheer natural fibers. They are the most compatible in appearance, and polyester thread is so strong that it could damage the delicate fabric in the event of a stitching problem.

Stitch a test sample, and check to make sure that a generous amount of top thread appears on the reverse side of the fabric. Loosen the top tension if needed to allow more thread to flow to the back of the fabric. On satin stitches, there should be a ratio of at least two-thirds top thread and one-third bobbin thread, and it's acceptable on this fabric to have almost no bobbin thread showing. You can wind your bobbin with thread that matches the top thread for an aesthetically pleasing result. In most cases, if using rayon or cotton embroidery thread, the same thread used for the top thread type may be wound onto the bobbin. Tone-on-tone color selection is appealing on sheer fabrics, and matching thread color to background color can help keep the stitch count to a minimum.

DESIGN PROPERTIES

Running stitches and satin stitches are quite well-suited to sheer fabrics. With these stitch types, the top thread tensions can be set to run very light, allowing top thread to flow to the back of the fabric. Fill-stitched areas have a greater concentration of stitches that may be harder for the fabric to support. Whenever possible, select, create, or edit your design to contain the fewest needle penetrations possible. Reduce risk to your delicate fabric and creates less weight, helping to maintain its natural drape.

For satin and fill-stitched areas you will need to test your specific fabric for the most appropriate density setting. Don't be afraid to use settings that are lighter than normal because you will be surprised how much they complement the fabric. Try a 4.5 or 5.0 point (0.45mm or 0.5mm) density for satins and fill areas and test. If you don't have the ability to alter density settings, enlarge the design so that the distance between the stitches will be increased. This will result in a softer design that is less stressful to the fabric.

Don't place too many stitches in a small area on a sheer fabric, such as in curves and corners. Some embroidery software has an option to "clean up", or remove stitches that are smaller than a specific threshold measurement, which is usually smaller than the width of your needle (fig. 9-7). If you have this option, use it, because these stitches won't affect the appearance of your design, while removing them helps to maintain the structure of delicate fabrics.

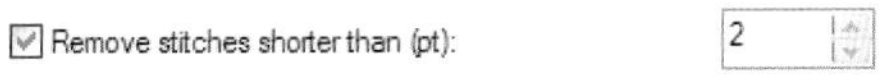

☑ Remove stitches shorter than (pt):   2

Fig. 9-7. Remove stitches that are too small to benefit the appearance of your design and that could cause thread breaks or damage your delicate sheer fabric.

Stitching and Finishing Tips
for Natural-Fiber Sheers

Trim any connecting threads and jump stitches that will not be a part of the finished design before other stitches travel over the top of them. You don't want to dig out these stitches later, which could cause damage to the fabric.

Trim all excess threads from the front and the back of your fabric because thread tails are visible through a sheer fabric and must be removed (fig. 9-6).

Gently pull away the stabilizer, holding your thumb and forefinger next to the edge of the embroidery. If you wish to remove any trace of stabilizer, and your fabric is washable, soak it in water or wash to remove the remaining stabilizer. Press the fabric using a pressing cloth.

SYNTHETIC-FIBER SHEER CURTAIN

RECOMMENDATIONS

Needle
Size 65/9 or 70/10 sharp point

Stabilizer

Just as with natural-fiber sheer fabrics, the best choice is a transparent stabilizer. If you select your design carefully, set very light tensions, and are working on a somewhat crisp sheer fabric, you may be able to fine-tune your settings to work without a stabilizer.

This technique requires testing and practice, but it is achievable with light stitch-count designs. In the chapter on knits, organza was recommended as a stabilizer for open knits, so it is capable of supporting embroidery stitches on its own when the elements are carefully balanced. Midweight water-soluble stabilizers are a reliable base for synthetic sheers. A single layer of 35-micron midweight water-soluble will support light to midrange stitch count designs.

Tissue paper is a good support base when stitching seams on some sheer fabrics, and it may be suitable as a light stabilizer on certain sheer fabrics with small simple solid shapes, such as dots. It tears away cleanly if the design is solid enough and there aren't places where small bits will remain trapped.

Hooping

The same general hooping guidelines apply for synthetic sheer fabrics as were described in the section on natural fiber sheers, but there are a couple of additional points to keep in mind. When you are assembling a sewn project that has embroidery, it's best to embroider the fabric before cutting out the pattern. Cutting first could result in excessive fraying of the fabric along the

Synthetic Sheers

Characteristics
Synthetic sheers are often made from polyester or nylon. They may be crisp, like organza, or drapey, like chiffon.

Challenges
Synthetic sheer fabrics are made from strong fibers that require clean needle penetration, light tensions, and invisible support.

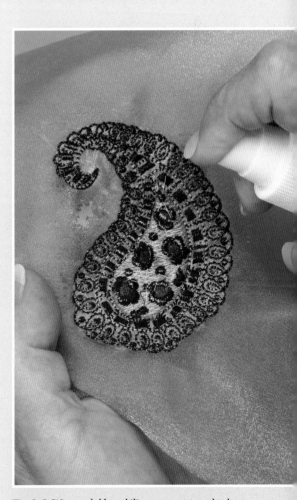

Fig. 9-8. Water-soluble stabilizers may not need to be removed completely depending on the item's use. If appropriate, just pull away the excess.

cut edges during embroidery. Place the pattern piece or pieces that will be embroidered on the fabric and trace around them using chalk or disappearing marker, and remove the pattern. This allows you to place your embroidery appropriately without the risk of fraying.

Synthetic sheer fabrics have a tendency to twist and get "off-grain" during the hooping process. Watch the fabric closely as you place it in the hoop, keeping the grain as straight as possible. For this reason, it is desirable to mark the grain using a chalk wheel or other method before beginning the hooping process. Before placing the hoop into the machine, check the back to be sure the stabilizer extends beyond all edges of the hoop.

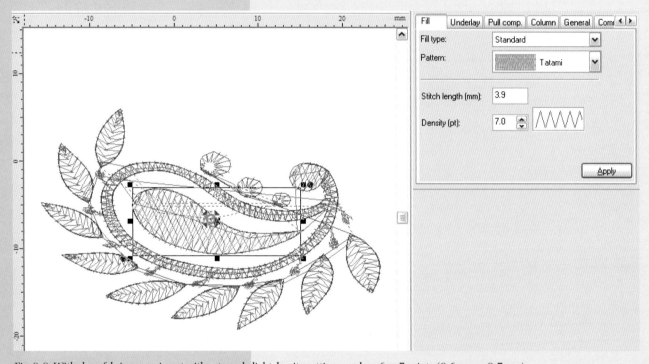

Fig. 9-9. With sheer fabrics, experiment with extremely light density settings, such as 6 or 7 points (0.6mm or 0.7mm).

DESIGN PROPERTIES

Light densities on satin and fill-stitched areas are best, and open airy fills are wonderful on sheers (fig. 9-9). In fact, on commercially made items such as sheer drapes, the fill areas are frequently programmed as running stitches in a pattern that resembles a fill stitch.

The main rule for sheers in programming is simplicity. Minimalism extends to number of colors as well as stitch count. This doesn't mean that a design needs to appear skimpy; rather, it should be light and in keeping with the fabric's characteristics (fig. 9-10).

Fig. 9-10. Many designs can be modified for use on sheers by simplifying colors and outlines and using lighter densities.

The enclosed CD contains the designs

used on the projects featured in this book. The CD contains the original design files, which were digitized for normal fabrics, and digitized files that have been modified to suit the fabric types covered in chapters five through nine. See Design Details on CD for directory.

The original files use the standard default settings for density, underlay, and stitch length. To make the files suitable for other fabric types, I modified the settings in my embroidery software. I began by modifying according to my experience in working with a specific fabric type, and then I stitched a sample. In many cases, further modifications were made following the sample stitch-out.

For example, I know that when stitching on a pile fabric, I must add underlay stitches to secure the topping. The underlay also serves the purpose of preventing "pokies"—bits of the pile poking through the thread after many washings. These settings often worked out the first time.

On the other hand, I added underlay and density to the design used on the bulky knit to get good coverage. Interestingly enough, in my test stitching, I discovered that I needed to increase the pull compensation value so that the satin stitches would meet the outlines. I also had to lighten the satin density to about 6 points (0.6mm) because the heavier density was pushing the knit too much, even with a topping. This was a total surprise, but the spongy bulky knit did not handle the added density well, and the heavy stitching did not lay into the knit well.

You can load the original design files and any of the specially modified design files into your embroidery software for a comparison. In some instances, details were omitted from a design. For example, the Zebra Paisley used on the sheer curtain project (page 112) was stripped of all but its most basic elements before being applied to the wispy, peach-colored fabric.

In other instances, pull compensation was added to help fill or satin-stitched areas meet with the outlines. While you can't detect this setting in your embroidery software, you may be able to see the expanded shapes on your computer monitor.

Within your embroidery software, you should be able to see the differences in:

- stitch count
- underlay types
- stitch lengths
- density settings

While a few settings may surprise you, most of the settings follow a logic that is somewhat parallel to sewing on that specific fabric type. As you study different examples, you can test your own stitch logic by editing designs in your library to be suitable for a specific fabric type. Remember that your best guess is still just a guess, and there is no substitute for a test stitch-out. If you always do a test, you will never be disappointed in your final result, and you will usually learn something. I hope this CD will help you learn more about the settings suitable for special fabric types.

Formats on the CD support all popular home embroidery models. Use of designs on the CD requires a computer to transfer the designs to the media type accepted by your machine.

Formats included are:

BabyLock: PES	Singer: CSD, EMD, XXX
Bernina: ART2, ART5, PES	Toyota-Aisin POEM/
Brother: PES	Viking: CSD, HUS, VIP
Elna: SEW, JEF, EMD	Simplicity: PES
Janome: SEW, JEF	White: PES
Kenmore: SEW, JEF	Universal - DST, EXP
Pfaff: PCS, VIP	

Fabric	Needle Flat Shank	Needle Round Shank	Stabilizer	Comments
Silk Charmeuse	Sharp Point Microtex (H-M) 70/10 Universal (H) 75/11 Sharp (H-J) size 70/10	Sharp or acute round (SPI) 65/9 or 70/10	2 layers of medium weight tear-away	Protect and cushion with layer of tissue between the fabric and hoop. Tear window where embroidery will be applied.
Lycra Spandex and other multi-directional stretch fabric	Light ball point (HE) 75/11 Medium ball point (H-SUK) size 70/10	Light ball point (SES) or medium all point (SUK) 65/9, 70/10, or 75/11	PolyMesh or Fusible PolyMesh	Items that will be stretched when worn should be stretched slightly when hooping.
Broadcloth or Poplin with Spandex	Sharp Point Microtex (H-M) 70/10 Universal (H) 75/11 Sharp (H-J) size 70/10	Sharp or acute round (SPI) 70/10 or 75/11	Fusible Polymesh or ShirtTailor by Pellon and lightweight crisp tear-away	Adhere the fusible cut-away to the reverse side of the fabric and hoop completely in hoop. Slide the crisp tear-away between hooped item and machine table.

Fabric	Needle Flat Shank	Needle Round Shank	Stabilizer	Comments
Natural Leather	Sharp point for thin or brittle leather Sharp(H-J) size 70/10 or 80/12; light ball point (H-E) for spongy leather size 75/11 or 80/12	Sharp point for thin or brittle leather (R) or (SPI) size 70/10 or 80/12 Light ball point (SES) for spongy leather size 75/11 or 80/12	a. Fusible Polymesh or ShirtTailor for thin brittle leather b. HydroStick or other water-activated tear-away for substantial leather c. Medium cut-away	Adhere leather to stabilizer whenever possible. If not possible, cutaway stabilizer is recommended.
Vinyl	Thin vinyl:Sharp (H-J) size 70/10 or 80/12 Thick or bonded vinyl: light ball point (H-E) size 75/11 or 80/12	Thin vinyl Sharp (R) 70/10 or 80/12 Thick or bonded vinyl Light ball point (SES) size 75/11 or 80/12	Water-activated tear-away stabilizer or adhere conventional stabilizer with embroidery spray adhesive	Adhering vinyl to a stabilizer can minimize its tendency to stretch.
Sheer Fabrics – Natural and Synthetic Fibers	Sharp Point Microtex (H-M) 65/9 or 70/10 Universal (H) 75/11 Sharp (H-J) size 70/10	Sharp or acute round (SPI) 65/9 or 70/10	a. one or two layers of midweight (35 microns) water soluble stabilizer where transparency is needed b. crisp tear-away for solid designs where transparency is not an issue	Never tug sheer fabric after hooping. Use transparent stabilizer beneath the fabric for lettering or other designs with open areas that allow stabilizer to show through.

Fabric	Needle Flat Shank	Needle Round Shank	Stabilizer	Comments
Lightweight Knits	Light ball point (H-E) size 70/10 or 75/11	Light ball point (SES) size 70/10 or 75/11	Cut-away stabilizer PolyMesh type	Hoop stabilizer completely in hoop for proper support.
Bulky Knits	Medium ballpoint (H-SUK)	Medium ballpoint (SUK)	Polyester organza in matching color with midweight water-soluble topping	Hoop all three layers together.
Gauze Fabric	Sharp (H-J) size 70/10 or Universal (H) size 70/10 or 75/11	Sharp (R) size 70/10 or 75/11 or light ball point (SES) size 70/10 or 75/11	Midweight or heavy-weight water-soluble beneath fabric, light-weight water-soluble topping.	Hoop all three layers together.
Lightweight Nylon	Sharp (H-J) size 70/10 Universal (H) size 70/10 or 75/11 Embroidery Needle (H-E) size 75/11	Sharp (R) size 70/10 or 75/11 or light ball point (SES) size 70/10 or 75/11	Medium weight crisp tear-away (1½ to 2 ounce) in multiple layers if needed	Float additional layers between hooped item and machine table if puckering is detected while stitching.

Fabric	Needle Flat Shank	Needle Round Shank	Stabilizer	Comments
Stiff Nylon	Sharp (H-J) size 90/14 or Embroidery Needle (H-E) Size 90/14	Sharp (R) size 80/12 or 90/14	Medium weight (1½ ounce to 2 ounce) crisp tear-away, single layer	Stabilizer helps fabric glide, especially coated nylon
Polyester Satin	Universal (H) size 70/10 or Embroidery needle (HE) size 75/11	Light ball point (SES) size 70/10 or 75/11	Light to medium weight (1 to 2 ounce.) crisp tear-away, single or multiple layers	Hooped stabilizer in with fabric, but slide additional layer(s) between hoop and machine bed if puckering is detected during embroidery.
Velvet	Embroidery needle (H-E) size 75/11	SES Light ball point size 75/11	One or more layers of light- or mid-weight crisp tear-away beneath the fabric	Topping should be pulled away following underlay stitching, prior to final layer of stitching to avoid need for water or heat for removal.
Terry Cloth	Embroidery needle (H-E) size 75/11	SES Light ball point size 75/11	Medium-weight tear-away (1½ ounce to 2 ounce), water-soluble topping or permanent topping	Alternate method: Fuse Totally Stable to back of terry and adhere to self-adhesive stabilizer base. Remove both after completion of embroidery. Topping is also recommended.

Fabric	Needle Flat Shank	Needle Round Shank	Stabilizer	Comments
Pile Fleece	Embroidery Needle (H-E) size 75/11	SES Light Ball Point size 75/11	Cut-away stabilizer PolyMesh type or medium-weight soft tear-away for small, simple designs; light or medium weight water-soluble based on height of pile	Alternate method: Adhere pile to base of self-adhesive stabilizer for small, simple designs or lettering. Topping is also recommended.
Faux Fur	Embroidery Needle (H-E) size 75/11	SES Light Ball Point size 75/11	Medium-weight soft tear-away or heavy-weight water-soluble below fur; medium-weight (35 micron) water-soluble topping	Alternate method: Adhere pile to base of self-adhesive stabilizer. Topping is also recommended.

NEEDLES

www.embroideryonline.com

This resource has round shank and flat shank needles in a variety of sizes, including titanium coated needles

www.euronotions.com

A distributor of Schmetz needles.

HOOPING STATION

HoopMate

www.abcemb.com

This easel-style stand is designed to hold your outer hoop and stabilizer while hooping, and to assist with placement. Available with holders for home, commercial or semi-commercial machines.

PLACEMENT AIDS

Perfect Placement Kit

Designs in Machine Embroidery
www.dzgns.com
2517 Manana Drive
Dallas, TX 75220
888-739-0555

A clear ruler plus 15 plastic templates for linens and garments, target stickers for marking placement and printed color instruction book.

Embroiderer's Buddy and Embroiderer's Little Buddy

www.abcemb.com

Right-angle ruler guides for accurate placement on shirts, jackets and other items.

MAGNETIC HOOPING SYSTEM

Magna Hoop System

Designs in Machine Embroidery
www.dzgns.com
2517 Manana Drive
Dallas, TX 75220
888-739-0555

Five frame sizes and four magnets for use with base plate that fits inside your embroidery hoop.

SELF-ADHESIVE HOLDING SYSTEM

Hoop-It-All

Hoop-It-All, Inc.
7200 E. 2nd St., Bldg. A
Prescott Valley, AZ 86314-2208
800-947-4911

Handy holder used as a carrier for self-adhesive stabilizer, used in place of a two-part hoop. Available for home embroidery machines.

GARMENT LEATHER FOR TEST STITCH-OUTS

Tandy Leather Factory

www.tandyleatherfactory.com
Tandy Leather Factory, Inc.
Attn: Sales
3847 East Loop 820 South
Fort Worth, TX 76119
800-433-3201

Order the Premium Upholstery Remnant Package for one pound of leather remnants.

MESH CUTAWAY STABILIZERS

Translucent lightweight backing is highly stable and available in a variety of widths, colors and specialty styles.

OESD PolyMesh
    www.embroideryonline.com to order or for dealers
    Available in white, beige, black, fusible and pressure-sensitive.

Floriani No Show Mesh
    www.rnkdistributing.com for dealers
    Available in white, beige and fusible.

SELF-ADHESIVE STABILIZERS

Stabilizer with self-adhesive coating that is safe for use with home and commercial embroidery machines.

Sulky Sticky Plus
    www.speedstitch.com or
    www.sulky.com for dealers

Floriani Perfect Stick
    www.rnkdistributing.com for dealers

Stick It All
    Hoop-It-All, Inc.
    7200 E. 2nd St., Bldg. A
    Prescott Valley, AZ 86314-2208
    (800) 947-4911

HEAT-REMOVABLE TOPPINGS AND STABILIZERS

Clear film stabilizer removed with heat. May be used above or below the fabric.

Sulky Heat Away Clear Film
    www.speedstitch.com or
    www.sulky.com for dealers

Floriani Heat n' Gone
    www.rnkdistributing.com for dealers

PERMANENT TOPPINGS

Use a color to coordinate with the embroidery thread for a permanent mask for contrasting fabric colors or deeply textured fabrics.

Simply Stable Hide It
    www.abcemb.com

Cover Up
    www.hoopitall.com
    Hoop-It-All, Inc.
    7200 E. 2nd St., Bldg. A
    Prescott Valley, AZ 86314-2208
    (800) 947-4911

LIGHT-TACK TEMPORARY FUSIBLE TEARAWAYS

Heat-fusible stabilizer that is easily removed. Ideal for use as a buffer between fabric and more aggressive adhesive stabilizers.

Totally Stable
  www.speedstitch.com or
  www.sulky.com for dealers
Fa-Bond
  www.hoopitall.com
  Hoop-It-All, Inc.
  7200 E. 2nd St., Bldg. A
  Prescott Valley, AZ 86314-2208
  (800) 947-4911

WATER-ACTIVATED ADHESIVE STABILIZERS

Water-activated adhesive on these stabilizers is dry after application for no sticky build-up on needles.

HydroStick Tearaway or Cutaway
  www.embroideryonline.com to order or
  for dealers
Floriani Wet n Stick Tearaway or Cutaway
  www.rnkdistributing.com for dealers

WATER-SOLUBLE TOPPINGS OR STABILIZERS

Clear film stabilizers used above fabric to create a smooth embroidery surface, or below fabric as a base.

Lightweight Clear Film, approximately 20
  microns:
  www.embroideryonline.com to order or
  for dealers
  www.speedstitch.com or
  www.sulky.com for dealers
  www.rnkdistributing.com for dealers
Midweight Clear Film, approximately 35
  microns:
  www.speedstitch.com or
  www.sulky.com for dealers
Heavyweight Clear Film, over 50 microns:
  www.embroideryonline.com to order or
  for dealers
  www.speedstitch.com or
  www.sulky.com for dealers

MESH TYPE STABILIZERS

Water-soluble stabilizer for use under fabric where a firm base is needed.

AquaMesh
www.embroideryonline.com to order or for
  dealers
Wet n Gone
  www.rnkdistributing.com for dealers
  Available in plain, fusible and self-
  adhesive varieties.

Machine Embroidery Wild & Wacky

Stitch on Any and Every Surface

LINDA GRIEPENTROG AND REBECCA KEMP BRENT

Go beyond machine embroidery basics using unique bases such as wood and canvas, and techniques including embossing and painting, and apply to 28 projects and 40 exclusive designs on a CD-ROM.

paperback, 128 pages, 225 color photos
ISBN 13: 978-0-89689-277-4
ISBN: 0-89689-277-8
MEWA

Machine Embroidery on Paper

ANNETTE GENTRY BAILEY

This exciting reference takes machine embroidery into paper crafts with 30+ cool embroidered projects including cards, frames, boxes and sachets. Features 20 original embroidery designs on an enclosed CD-ROM.

paperback, 48 pages, 115+ color photos
ISBN 13: 978-0-89689-302-3
ISBN: 0-89689-302-2
MEPP

Contemporary Machine-Embroidered Accessories

Transform Everyday Accessories into Designer Originals

EILEEN ROCHE

Discover valuable secrets for using stabilizers and creating 18 exciting projects you can make and wear, including hats, scarves, belts, gloves and more, regardless of your size.

paperback, 128 pages, 250 color photos
ISBN 13: 978-0-89689-491-4
ISBN: 0-89689-491-6
Z0762

More Embroidery Machine Essentials

How to Customize, Edit and Create Decorative Designs

JEANINE TWIGG

From combining decorative designs to stitch editing to creating designs, Jeanine Twigg provides basic software theories and instructions that can be used with any embroidery machine. Includes a CD of 10 exclusive designs and artwork.

paperback, 128 pages, 150+ color photos
ISBN 13: 978-0-87349-439-7
ISBN: 0-87349-439-3
MSTIT

Digitizing Made Easy

Create Custom Embroidery Designs Like a Pro

JOHN DEER

Explore time-tested methods, explained in 250 step-by-step photos, for mastering the tools and techniques of modern digitizing, and adding your own personal character to any project.

paperback, 128 pages, 250 color photos
ISBN 13: 978-0-89689-492-1
ISBN: 0-89689-492-4
Z0763